What Does It Mean
to Be Saved?

WHAT DOES IT MEAN TO BE SAVED?

BROADENING EVANGELICAL HORIZONS OF SALVATION

John G. Stackhouse, Jr., editor

Baker Academic
A Division of Baker Book House Co

Published by Baker Academic
a division of Baker Book House Company
P.O. Box 6287, Grand Rapids, MI 49516-6287

Printed in the United States of America

Library of Congress Cataloging-in-Publication Data

What does it mean to be saved? : broadening evangelical horizons of salvation / John G. Stackhouse, Jr., editor.
    p.   cm.
    Includes bibliographical references and indexes.
    ISBN 0-8010-2353-X (pbk.)
    1. Salvation. 2. Evangelicalism. I. Stackhouse, John Gordon.
BT752.W52 2002
234—dc21   2002066617

For information about Baker Academic, visit our web site:
www.bakeracademic.com

Contents

Contributors   7
Preface   9
JOHN G. STACKHOUSE, JR.

Part 1   Basic Reconsiderations
1   The New Exodus/New Creational Restoration
of the Image of God: A Biblical-Theological
Perspective on Salvation   15
RIKK E. WATTS
2   "Let Us See Thy Great Salvation": What Did It
Mean to Be Saved for the Early Evangelicals?   43
D. BRUCE HINDMARSH
3   *Agnus Victor:* The Atonement as Victory
and Vicarious Punishment   67
HENRI A. G. BLOCHER

Part 2   Expanding Particular Zones
4   What Is *This Life* For? Expanding Our View
of Salvation   95
VINCENT BACOTE
5   Being Saved as a New Creation: Co-Humanity
in the True *Imago Dei*   115
CHERITH FEE NORDLING
6   Salvation as Life in the (New) City   137
AMY L. SHERMAN
7   Christians Should Be Converted Pagans: The
Apologetic Problem of a Gospel That Denies
Our Earthiness   153
LOREN WILKINSON

Part 3   **Responses**

8   What's Evangelical about Evangelical
     Soteriology?   179
     JOHN WEBSTER

9   Clarifying Vision, Empowering Witness   185
     JONATHAN R. WILSON

     Subject Index   195
     Scripture Index   199

Contributors

Vincent Bacote (Ph.D., Drew University) is Assistant Professor of Theology at Wheaton College. He is the author of articles that have appeared in books and magazines, including *The Gospel in Black and White* (InterVarsity) and *re:generation quarterly.*

Henri A. G. Blocher (D.D., Gordon-Conwell Theological Seminary) is Doyen Honoraire and Professor of Systematic Theology at the Faculté Libre de Théologie Evangélique, Vaux-sur-Seine, France. His publications include *Evil and the Cross: Christian Thought and the Problem of Evil* (Apollos/Inter-Varsity) and *Original Sin: Illuminating the Riddle* (Apollos/Inter-Varsity).

D. Bruce Hindmarsh (D.Phil., University of Oxford) is the James M. Houston Associate Professor of Spiritual Theology at Regent College. He is the author of *John Newton and the English Evangelical Tradition* (Oxford University Press).

Cherith Fee Nordling (Ph.D. candidate, University of St. Andrews) has several essays in the process of publication and is the coauthor of *The Pocket Dictionary of Theological Terms* (InterVarsity).

Amy L. Sherman (Ph.D., University of Virginia) is Senior Fellow at the Welfare Policy Center of the Hudson Institute. She also serves as Urban Ministries Advisor at Trinity Presbyterian Church in Charlottesville, Virginia. She is the author of four books, including *Restorers of Hope: Reaching the Poor in Your Community with Church-based Ministries That Work* (Crossway).

7

John G. Stackhouse, Jr. (Ph.D., University of Chicago) is Sangwoo Youtong Chee Professor of Theology and Culture at Regent College. He has written and edited several books, including *Evangelical Futures: A Conversation on Theological Method* (Baker Academic) and *No Other Gods before Me? Evangelicals and the Challenge of World Religions* (Baker Academic).

Rikk E. Watts (Ph.D., University of Cambridge) is Associate Professor of New Testament at Regent College. In addition to a number of articles, he has written *Isaiah's New Exodus and Mark* (Mohr Siebeck and Baker Academic).

John Webster (Ph.D., University of Cambridge) is Lady Margaret Professor of Divinity at the University of Oxford and Canon of Christ Church. He is the author of a number of books on modern theology and dogmatics, most recently *Word and Church* (Continuum).

Loren Wilkinson (Ph.D., Syracuse University) is Professor of Interdisciplinary Studies at Regent College. His books include *Earthkeeping in the Nineties: Christian Stewardship of Natural Resources* (Eerdmans).

Jonathan R. Wilson (Ph.D., Duke University) is Professor of Religious Studies at Westmont College in Santa Barbara, California. He is the author of several books, most recently *God So Loved the World: A Christology for Disciples* (Baker Academic).

Preface

JOHN G. STACKHOUSE, JR.

This book shouldn't be necessary.

In his gracious but penetrating response to the essays in this volume, Oxford professor John Webster wonders whether it is particularly North American evangelicals who need to be reminded that the Bible presents salvation as offering more than getting souls to heaven. My experience of teaching soteriology for several years at Regent College—an international graduate school of Christian studies whose students come from thirty-five countries on every continent except Antarctica—leads me to think that evangelicals far and wide also need their horizons expanded. Over and over, students have betrayed an understanding of salvation that amounted to a sort of spiritual individualism that is little better than Gnosticism. (It is better in that at least they believed God loves the whole world, not just the élite few.)

In the light of this troubling experience, shared by others at Regent and our colleagues elsewhere, Regent College hosted a conference in October 2001 that presented scholars who could open up new vistas for such evangelicals. We did not seek to produce a coherent and comprehensive doctrine of salvation. Instead, for the conference and for this resulting book, we deliberately invited specialists from a wide range of backgrounds (biblical studies, church history, historical theology, systematic theology, philosophy, literature, and political science); various countries (Canada, the United States, the United Kingdom, Australia, and France); diverse confessions (Pentecostal, Baptist,

Presbyterian, Anglican, and Methodist); and different career positions (from Ph.D. candidates to distinguished professors). We could not be all-inclusive, of course, and our strenuous attempts to include participants from the Two-Thirds World were frustrated at every turn. Still, what is offered here does fit the bill: This is a collection of pointed essays intended to prod evangelical theology out of its comfortable spiritual individualism and toward a vision of salvation as large as God's mission to the world he loves and redeems.

This book ought to be unnecessary also because so many theologians have worked over these themes before. There is not much in this volume that the authors themselves would claim to be utterly original. But the fact that so little of this theological breadth and richness seems to be penetrating to the pews of international evangelicalism should provoke professors of theology and pastors of churches to redouble our efforts to teach what the Bible teaches about salvation in all its glorious complexity and scope.

In fact, we could make an important start simply by teaching that salvation is *not* about "Christians going to heaven." Salvation is about God redeeming the whole earth. Salvation is about Christians—and perhaps others, also saved by the work of Christ but perhaps not knowing about him in this life—heading home to the God they love and the company of all the faithful. Salvation is about heading for the New Jerusalem, not heaven: a garden city on earth, not the very abode of God and certainly not a bunch of pink clouds in the sky. Salvation is not about the mental cartoons drawn by medieval illustrators and found in *Far Side* comic strips. It is about the splendid collage of images offered up in the wealth of biblical glimpses of what is to come. And salvation is not only about what is to come but also about what is ours to enjoy and foster here and now.

These essays prompt us to think in these larger, more vivid, and more exciting ways. They lead us out of our narrow and rather boring views of salvation into resplendent landscapes of God's re-creative power and love. They expand our minds, warm our hearts, and move our hands to participate with God in his great, worldwide mission.

In doing all of that, then, perhaps this book is necessary after all!

In convening the conference behind this book, I am grateful for the advice and assistance of the following colleagues: Peter Quek, sometime conference coordinator at Regent College; Bill Reimer, manager of Regent's bookstore; Stan Grenz, professor at Carey Theological College and Regent College; and Bob Hosack, editor at Baker Academic. I am glad to acknowledge the financial assistance of Regent College, Baker Academic, and the Social Sciences and Humanities Research Council of Canada in putting on this conference and supporting my work in editing the subsequent volume. Melinda Van Engen lent her firm and graceful touch to editing the book for Baker Academic. Elizabeth Powell assisted me in my various responsibilities with, as always, competence and cheerfulness, and also compiled the index. In such good company, in such good work, I have enjoyed something of God's salvation.

Part I
Basic Reconsiderations

I

The New Exodus/ New Creational Restoration of the Image of God

A Biblical-Theological Perspective on Salvation

RIKK E. WATTS

How often has one heard it said, "I can't help it. I'm only human"? Our humanness is somehow seen at best as a liability and at worst as a besetting affliction. The great hope then for many evangelicals is to be delivered from this existence to a higher state of glorious otherworldly bliss. I want to suggest that our ambivalence about our humanity derives in large part from a failure to appreciate a truly biblical understanding of salvation. If there is a central thrust to the concept of salvation, it must include at or near its center the idea of the new exodus/new creational restoration of our embodied humanity as the image of God and concomitant upon that the restoration of this creation in which God has placed us.

Given that this paper emerges from a theology conference and that Western theology has traditionally employed a particular set of categories in its discussions, some brief preliminary remarks on the nature of the material examined herein are needed.

First, as Martin Heidegger once argued, our experience of the present and expectations of the future can be constructed only from the materials of the past. This is certainly the case in regard to the Bible, whose Old and New Testaments from Genesis to Revelation are profoundly shaped by Israel's memory of the exodus.[1] But this is not all. Long ago Herman Gunkel, noting how 2 Peter 3:6–7 describes the final judgment in terms of the Genesis flood and how Matthew 24:37 likens the days of the coming of the Son of man to those of Noah, argued that from the biblical perspective, *Endzeit* (the last days) recapitulates *Urzeit* (prehistory).[2] Several scholars have recently developed this view, arguing that if there is a center to biblical theology, it is the concept of new creation; as the *Epistle of Barnabas* 6.13 states, "Behold I make the last things like the first things."[3] Put in more aphoristic terms, eschatology recapitulates protology. Furthermore, the imagery of Israel standing in the darkness before the sea, the fiery pillar bringing light, and the wind-driven emergence of dry land portrays the exodus as a recapitulation of creation (Exod. 14:19–21; Gen. 1:2–9).[4] Israel's founding moment of redemption from Egypt is a new creation. We should not be surprised, therefore, that when the prophets speak of Israel's new exodus from Babylonian exile, they too use the lan-

1. E.g., Y. Zakovitch, *The Concept of the Exodus in the Bible* (Jerusalem: Magnes, 1991); and the overview in Rikk E. Watts, "Exodus," in *The New Dictionary of Biblical Theology* (Downers Grove, Ill.: InterVarsity; Leicester: InterVarsity, 2000), 478–87.

2. *Schöpfung und Chaos in Urzeit und Endzeit* (Göttingen, 1895).

3. Greg K. Beale, "The Eschatological Conception of New Testament Theology," in *"The Reader Must Understand": Eschatology in Bible and Theology*, ed. K. E. Brower and M. W. Elliott (Leicester: Apollos, 1997), 11–52; and earlier William J. Dumbrell, *The End of the Beginning* (Homebush West, NSW: Lancer, 1985); and idem, *The Search for Order* (Grand Rapids: Baker, 1994).

4. See Rikk E. Watts, "On the Edge of the Millennium: Making Sense of Genesis 1," in *Living in the Lamblight: Christianity and Contemporary Challenges to the Gospel*, ed. Hans Boersma (Vancouver: Regent College Publishing, 2001), 143.

guage of new creation[5] and that the New Testament therefore describes Jesus' fulfillment of Israel's restorationist hopes using new exodus/new creation motifs.[6] From a biblical-theological perspective, eschatology is fundamentally about a new exodus/ new creation. Consequently, this paper takes its primary bearings from these two constellations of memories.

Second, these founding moment memories have no shape apart from the matrix of the traditions of the society in which they were formed and transmitted.[7] As such they naturally employ the icons, images, and symbols of their day as they mark out Israel's identity as Yahweh's people over against the myths and ideologies of the surrounding cultures.[8] Two considerations emerge for this discussion. Although common fare in the ancient Near East, these ways of conceptualizing reality are unusual, to say the least, to moderns, and we can easily miss both the imagery and its significance. For many, including theologians and even New Testament scholars who are unfamiliar with recent prodigious advances in understanding, this might be an utterly unfamiliar way of thinking, and it may take some time to get accustomed to it. I encourage you, therefore, to reserve judgment until the entire picture emerges, allowing the coherence of the whole to make its own case.

Because we moderns are more at home in the world of Socratic logic, the pictorial and metaphoric discourse of the ancient Near East might seem too imprecise and fluid to be of significant help in a tradition much given to closely argued distinctions. But there are strengths to the pre-Socratic ways. Metaphor by its very nature combines a sense of limitation and focus with a sense of the indeterminate and mysterious. It helps us to see more clearly and at

5. Most notably in Isaiah. See B. W. Anderson, "Exodus Typology in Second Isaiah," in *Israel's Prophetic Heritage,* ed. B. W. Anderson and W. Harrelson (New York: Harper, 1962), 177–95; C. Stuhlmueller, *Creative Redemption in Deutero-Isaiah,* Analecta biblica 43 (Rome: Pontifical Biblical Institute, 1970).

6. This new exodus conception is fundamental to N. T. Wright's return-from-exile conception of Jesus. See his *Jesus and the Victory of God* (Minneapolis: Fortress, 1996); see also Watts, "Exodus," and on new creation, the authors cited in footnote 3 above.

7. W. Pannenberg, ed., *Revelation as History* (London: Sheed and Ward, 1969), 152–53.

8. P. Ricoeur, "The Function of Fiction in Shaping Reality," *Man and World* 12 (1979): 123–41; J. Ellul, "Le rôle médiateur de l'idéologie," in *Demythisation et idéologie,* ed. E. Castelli (Paris: Aubier, 1973), 335–54.

the same time intimates that there is yet more to see. As such it seems a particularly appropriate way of addressing the mystery of being human.

Since eschatology recapitulates protology, salvation cannot be properly understood apart from creation. This chapter begins, therefore, with creation, arguing that in keeping with ancient Near Eastern conceptualizations, the cosmos is seen as Yahweh's temple-palace, and the climax of creation is the installation of humanity as his "cult-idol" or image-bearer within it. It then maintains that the exodus from Egypt, Israel's return from exile, and God's new exodus/new creational work in Christ Jesus are best understood in terms of the restoration of the defaced image-bearer and consequently the restoration of the cosmos as Yahweh's temple-palace in which the newly Spirit-indwelt image-bearer is installed.

Creation: Yahweh's Temple-Palace and the Installation of His Image

Creation as the Formation of Yahweh's Temple-Palace

One of the striking features of the Hebrew Bible's conceptualization of creation is its thoroughgoing use of architectural imagery. In Job 38, Yahweh, the master builder of creation, questions Job:

> "Where were you when I laid the earth's foundation? . . .
> Who marked off its dimensions? Surely you know!
>   Who stretched a measuring line across it?
> On what were its footings set,
>   or who laid its cornerstone . . .
> Who shut up the sea behind doors . . .
> when I fixed limits for it
>   and set its doors and bars in place. . . .
> Have you entered the storehouses of the snow
>   or seen the storehouses of the hail?"
>
> vv. 4–6, 8, 10, 22

Other passages also speak of the foundations of the earth (2 Sam. 22:8, 16; Pss. 18:15; 82:5; 102:25; 104:5; Prov. 8:29; Isa. 24:18; 51:13, 16; Zech. 12:1; cf. 2 Sam. 22:8), the pillars of the earth and heavens (1 Sam. 2:8; Job 9:6; 26:11; Ps. 75:3), Yahweh laying out the beams of his upper chambers on the waters of the heavens (Ps. 104:3) and stretching out the heavens like a canopy/tent (Job 9:8; Pss. 102:25; 104:2; Isa. 40:12, 22; 42:5; 44:24; 45:12; 48:13; 51:13; Jer. 10:12; 31:37; 32:17; 51:15; Amos 9:6; Zech. 12:1), the windows (Gen. 7:11; 8:2; 2 Kings 7:2; Isa. 24:18; Mal. 3:10), and the storehouses of the heavens (Deut. 28:12; Jer. 10:13; 50:25; 51:16; cf. Job 38:22; Pss. 33:7; 135:7). Such passages clearly contain architectural metaphors.

But what kind of building is this? In keeping with a number of other ancient Near Eastern traditions in which the act of creation is construed as the building of a deity's temple-palace (temple and palace being the same word, הֵיכָל, in Hebrew),[9] Isaiah 66:1 has Yahweh declare, "Heaven is my throne and the earth is my footstool; what is the house which you would build for me?" and in language reminiscent of Genesis 2:2–3, "What is the place of my rest?" (RSV; cf. Pss. 11:4; 103:19; Micah 1:2–3). Where else does one find a throne and a footstool if not in a palace? And if that palace is the deity's, does that not mean that the whole of creation, the heavens *and* the earth, are Yahweh's temple? As Meredith Kline noted, the picture in Genesis 2:2–3 is that of Yahweh resting enthroned in his cosmic temple-palace.[10] Indeed, as Philo declared, "The whole universe must be regarded as the highest and, in truth, the holy temple of God" (*De Spec. Leg.* I 66).

Creation of Adam and Eve: The Image of Yahweh in His Temple-Palace

Katherine Beckerleg recently related the production of images of the gods in the ancient Near East to the Genesis account of the formation of Adam and Eve.[11] In terms of ancient prac-

9. In more detail, see Watts, "Genesis 1," 129–51, esp. 145–48.
10. *Kingdom Prologue* (private publication, 1993, Gordon-Conwell Theological Seminary, Sth. Hamilton, Mass.), 17–18, 23–26.
11. "The Formation, Animation, and Installation of the Images of the Gods in the ANE" (paper presented at the annual meeting of the Society of Biblical Literature, Orlando, Fla., November 1998); cf. Christopher Walker and Michael B. Dick, "The Induction of the Cult Image in Ancient Mesopotamia: The Mesopotamian *mis pi* Ritual," in *Born in Heaven Made on Earth: The Making of the Cult Image in the Ancient Near East* (Winona Lake, Ind.: Eisenbrauns, 1999), 74–83.

tice, first, the image would be formed, often in connection with sacred forests or gardens. This would be followed by a series of ritual acts of animation in which the eyes, ears, and mouth of the image would be opened, its limbs enabled, and the spirit of the deity invoked to indwell the image. As David Clines noted, this indwelling of the image by the fiery spirit of the deity was perhaps the crucial event since it was only when this occurred that the idol truly functioned as the deity's image.[12] Finally, the "enlivened" image was installed in its temple, where the deity could dwell among his people and daily provision could be made for his sustenance.

Now, if the climactic event was the installation of the image of the deity in its temple, and if we allow the creation-as-temple-palace metaphor, it is surely significant that on the last day of creation, the crowning moment occurs when Yahweh declares, "'Let us make humankind in our image, according to our likeness.' . . . So God created humankind in his image, in the image of God he created them; male and female he created them" (Gen. 1:26–27 NRSV). Furthermore, if Beckerleg is correct, the Genesis story is something of a polemic against contemporary idolatrous perspectives; instead of a "zoomorphic paganism" we have a "monotheistic anthropology."[13] We do not make a temple-palace for Yahweh; he has made one for us, and it is not only the earth in its entirety but Eden in particular. Hence the parallels between Eden and the tabernacle.[14] We do not form Yahweh in our image; he makes us in his. We do not "open" his eyes, ears, and so on; instead, he gives us sight, hearing, and ultimately fills us with his "breath." Nor do we provide for him; rather, he has done lavishly so for us. Well may the psalmist ask in wonder, "What are human beings that

12. "The Image of God in Man," *Tyndale Bulletin* 19 (1968): 53–103; cf. Gordon J. Wenham, *Genesis 1–15*, Word Biblical Commentary, vol. 1 (Waco: Word, 1987), 29–32.

13. See Crispin H. T. Fletcher-Louis, "God's Image, His Cosmic Temple, and the High Priest: Towards an Historical and Theological Account of the Incarnation" (unpublished paper, 2001), soon to be published in the Tyndale Lecture series; and John Kutzko, *Between Heaven and Earth: Divine Presence and Absence in Ezekiel*, Biblical and Judaic Studies UCSD 7 (Winona Lake, Ind.: Eisenbrauns, 2000).

14. G. J. Wenham, "Sanctuary Symbolism in the Garden of Eden Story," *Proceedings of the World Congress of Jewish Studies* 9 (1986): 19–25.

you are mindful of them? . . . You . . . crowned them with glory and honor" (Ps. 8:4–5 NRSV; cf. Ps. 8:3–9).

It is important to note that the image of the god was never intended to depict the deity's appearance but instead to describe elements of the function and attributes of the deity. Images were "probably pictograms rather than portraits."[15] Nevertheless, as is now widely recognized, the idea of image clearly involves its physicality: Our embodied form is also integral to our "functioning" as Yahweh's image in this physical world. Furthermore, far from being an inanimate object, the image was indwelt by the very life of the deity, such that the image became the primary focus of his presence on the earth (cf. Jer. 10:14; Hab. 2:19).[16]

According to this perspective, the biblical language indicates that all human beings—not just the Pharaohs of Egypt[17]—in their physicality, their maleness and femaleness, and their interplay between individual and collective, are intended to be living pictographs of Yahweh the Creator, enlivened by his breath (נְשָׁמָה) and ultimately by his indwelling Spirit (רוּחַ).[18] Our very embodied existence testifies to Yahweh's kingship, and our function and attributes should resemble his.[19] Just as Yahweh sits enthroned in his cosmic temple, so too humanity images him, reigning between his knees as it were in the smaller temple-palace of the earth and functioning as his vice-regents. As such we imitate to a lesser but faithful degree his ordering and filling of the cosmos in our ordering (or gardening) of the earth and our acts of filling it with other bearers of his

15. H. Frankfort, *Ancient Egyptian Religion* (New York: Harper & Bros., 1961), 12.

16. M. Lichtheim, *Ancient Egyptian Literature*, 3 vols. (Berkeley: University of California Press, 1973–78), 1:55; K. Bernhardt, *Gott und Bild* (Berlin: Karl Heinz, 1956); S. Morenz, *Egyptian Religion*, trans. A. Keep (Ithaca, N.Y.: Cornell University Press, 1973), 157; and A. L. Oppenheim, *Ancient Mesopotamia*, 2d ed. (Chicago: University of Chicago Press, 1977), 184.

17. The idea of the king representing the god, being his image on earth, appears to be largely an Egyptian idea found primarily around the time of the New Kingdom, though there are a few limited references to the idea in Mesopotamia.

18. The similarity of referents for these terms is evident in that they often occur in parallel (cf. Job 33:4; 34:14; Isa. 42:5; 57:16).

19. See, for example, Henri Blocher, *In the Beginning* (Leicester: Inter-Varsity, 1984), 79–94.

image.[20] (In terms of modern perspectives, to the extent that creation is seen as a place designed for the habitation of humanity, we are justified in seeing these ancient metaphors as a counterpart of the modern concept of the Anthropic Principle: The physical constants of the present cosmos seem finely tuned to the existence of humanity.)

It is imperative to understand what this means. As Jim Houston reminds us, although we are self-conscious beings, our destiny lies not in an individualistic self-fulfillment or self-glorification but in our conforming to the Other—namely, the God in whose image we are made.

The Fall and the Necessity of Salvation

The nexus of humans as bearers of Yahweh's image and yet subordinate to him comes to the fore at the Tree of the Knowledge of Good and Evil. At issue is whether humans will accept their subordinate status, recognizing only Yahweh as the final source of wisdom, or seek to usurp his prerogatives by trusting in their own ability to understand—that is, to fashion creation and even themselves in their own image and according to their own wisdom. The latter is, of course, tautologous. How can something make itself in its own image? Rejecting the one whose image we bear and whose "breath" we breathe necessarily leads to alienation from ourselves and our world and finally to death and dissolution. So begins the long descent into night characterized by Cain's murderous jealousy (Gen. 4:4–12), Lamech's abuse of judicial authority and women (he has two wives; Gen. 4:23–24), and finally the sons of the gods, self-actualizing heroes swollen to madness with arrogance under whom wickedness is unrestrained and by whom women, no longer companions, are reduced to objects of desire (Gen. 6:1–6).[21]

Creation too is bound up in this and suffers as a consequence of human rebellion (Gen. 3:17–18). The temple-palace and the bearer of the image fall together into ruin, and humanity finds itself driven farther away from the Garden until Cain, the crown

20. While writing this paper, I discovered that a similar view was being explored by Fletcher-Louis and am grateful for the stimulating discussions that ensued.

21. On the use of "gods" to describe the judicial/leadership roles of humans, see 2 Sam. 7:14; Pss. 2:7; 82.

prince, now finds himself in a desert land of wandering. Ultimately, in the flood the earth returns to its pre-creation state: formless and empty under the vast waters of the deep.

But even as Adam and Eve depart the Garden, in a striking demonstration of his future intention, Yahweh clothes them. Clothing in the ancient world carried far more significance than it does in the modern West, particularly the removal or donning of certain kinds of clothing, which in certain settings signified the loss or acquisition of throne rights.[22] In ancient Mesopotamia, for example, the Akkadian word "to cover" *(katamu)* also meant "to exercise power" such that for a monarch to take up a cloak meant the assumption of power (cf. David's disrobed dancing "before the Lord" as an expression of his submission to Yahweh's kingship; 2 Sam. 6:20–22).[23] Likewise, someone sold for a day as a slave would hand over his clothes or cloak, which marked him as a free man, to his creditors, thus signifying his bondage to them.[24] Understood in this way, Yahweh's gracious act of clothing insurrectionists Adam and Eve serves as the promissory guarantee that he will restore his image-bearers to their viceregent status[25] and so anticipates their return to their rightful place as Yahweh's cult-image in his temple-palace.

Exodus: Micro-re-creation and the Renewal of the Image

The related themes of creation and formation of the image can also be delineated in Israel's exodus. As already noted, the exodus it-

22. See Gordon Paul Hugenberger, *Marriage as a Covenant* (Leiden: Brill, 1994), 199, who cites L. R. Fisher et al., eds., *Ras Shama Parallels. The Texts from Ugarit and the Hebrew Bible*, II, *Analecta orientalia* 50 (1975): 122–215; cf. Genesis 37; Num. 20:24–28; 1 Kings 11:30–31; 19:19–21; Isa. 22:21; and M. Malul, *Studies in Mesopotamian Legal Symbolism*, Alter Orient und Altes Testament 221 (Kevekaer: Verlag Butzon & Bercker; Neukirchen-Vluyn: Neukirchener Verlag, 1988), 93ff. See also J. Schneider, "The Anthropology of Cloth," *Annual Review of Anthropology* 16 (1987): 409–48.

23. N. M. Waldman, "The Imagery of Clothing, Covering, and Over-powering," *Journal of the Ancient New Eastern Society of Columbia University* 19 (1989): 161–70.

24. Victor C. Matthews and Don C. Benjamin, *Social World of Ancient Israel 1250–587 BCE* (Peabody, Mass.: Hendrickson, 1993), 203.

25. Kline, *Kingdom*, 93–94, and the discussion therein on the covenantal significance of clothing another.

self constitutes an act of mini-(re)creation in which Israel learns
that it is not the gods of Egypt but Yahweh who is the Creator.[26]
Echoing and perhaps even informing the Genesis 1 account, at the
chaos sea of the end [of the ordered world] (i.e., יַם־סוּף), Yahweh
causes light to shine in the darkness and a wind (רוּחַ) to drive back
the chaotic waters of the deep, causing dry land to appear (Exod.
14:19–31; cf. Wis. 19:6).[27] Just as Yahweh earlier "rested" in the
great pavilion of his cosmos-temple-palace (cf. Psalm 93), so now he
comes to reside among his people in his glory-cloud over the tabernacle. This structure, like its later counterpart in Jerusalem, is itself
a microcosm reminding Israel that the whole cosmos is Yahweh's
temple-palace.[28] But even so, just as Yahweh created Eden, a special
place and a garden of delight, for humanity, bidding them to be
fruitful, so too he gives Israel, his new humanity, an Edenic land
flowing with milk and honey and promises them abundant fecundity (Exod. 3:8, 17). Here then is the beginning of a new creation.

Similarly, the constitution of Israel as Yahweh's covenant people can also be understood as a reformation of the image-bearer.
Israel is called Yahweh's son (Exod. 4:22), indicating a relationship that recalls the language of Adam, who fathered a son "in the
likeness of his image" (בִּדְמוּתוֹ כְּצַלְמוֹ [in his likeness, according to
his image], Gen. 5:3; cf. בְּצַלְמֵנוּ כִּדְמוּתֵנוּ [in our image, according to
our likeness], Gen. 1:26). In accepting and submitting to Torah, Israel repudiates the autonomy sought by Adam and Eve in the Garden. Along similar lines, the stylized tree of the seven-branched
candelabra and the tablets of the law in the tabernacle, in corresponding to the Tree of Life and the Tree of Knowledge of Good
and Evil, remind Israel that it is in obedience to Yahweh's Word
and in an existence centered on his presence that her true human-

26. Watts, "Genesis 1," 138–44.
27. Ibid., 143; and Bernard F. Batto, "Red Sea or Reed Sea?" *Biblical Arche-
ology Review* 10 (1984): 57–63.
28. Jon D. Levenson, *Theology of the Program of Restoration of Ezekiel 40–
48*, Harvard Semitic Monographs 10 (Cambridge, Mass.: Scholars Press,
1976); Susan Niditch, "Ezekiel 40–48 in a Visionary Context," *Catholic Biblical
Quarterly* 48 (1986): 208–48; Margaret Barker, *The Gate of Heaven: The History
and Symbolism of the Temple in Jerusalem* (London: SPCK, 1991); Ben F. Meyer,
"The Temple at the Navel of the Earth," in *Christus Faber: The Master-Builder
and the House of God* (Allison Park, Pa.: Pickwick, 1992), 217–79; and John F.
Kutsko, *Between Heaven and Earth: Divine Presence and Absence in the Book of
Ezekiel*, Biblical and Judaic Studies 7 (Winona Lake, Ind.: Eisenbrauns, 2000).

ity and life consist (Deut. 11:26; 30:11–20).[29] Likewise, the Torah-celebrating language of Psalm 19:7–8—"The law of the Lord is perfect, reviving the soul; the decrees of the Lord are sure, making wise the simple; the precepts of the Lord are right, rejoicing the heart; the commandment of the Lord is clear, enlightening the eyes" (NRSV)—seems a deliberate echo and thereby a deliberate repudiation of Eve's assessment of the tree in the Garden: "The woman saw that the tree was . . . a delight to the eyes, and . . . was to be desired to make one wise" (Gen. 3:6 NRSV).[30] The wisdom literature's frequent admonition that the fear of Yahweh is the beginning of wisdom also reflects this idea (Job 28:28; Ps. 111:10; Prov. 9:10). Echoing image language, reverence for Yahweh is the way in which Israel's eyes and ears are opened that the people might be filled with good things (Prov. 20:12 in respect of wisdom; cf. Isa. 50:4b–5a; 1:19). In the ancient Near East, the gods were recognized not by various physical traits or facial features but by the emblems they wore.[31] It might be this notion that lies behind Yahweh's command that his image-bearers bind his Word on their hands and between their eyes (Deut. 6:8; 11:18).

This conception of Israel as Yahweh's "idol/image" is at least in part what lies behind Ezekiel 16's comparison between Israel's fashioning and caring for her idols and Yahweh's fashioning and caring for Israel, interestingly enough, beginning at the exodus.[32] Recalling Yahweh's promissory act of covering Adam and Eve, one notes the particular emphasis on the lavish clothing he provides for his people (vv. 10–13, 16–18). A similar comparison is assumed in the anti-idol polemics of Isaiah 40–55, which mock Babylon's idols, who need to be formed, protected, and borne by humans, whereas Yahweh has formed Israel and protects and carries his people (Isa. 44:6–22; 46:1–13).[33]

But how is Israel to image Yahweh? Crispin Fletcher-Louis has proposed that in the ancient world "the symbolism of [the

29. Wenham, "Sanctuary."

30. D. J. A. Clines, "The Tree of Knowledge and the Law of Yahweh," *Vetus Testamentum* 24 (1974): 8–14.

31. C. J. Bleeker, *Hathor and Thoth* (Leiden: Brill, 1973), 23.

32. E.g., Ezek. 16:16–20; see further Fletcher-Louis, "God's Image," 4f.; cf. also Kutzko, *Between Heaven and Earth*.

33. Cf. R. J. Clifford, "The Function of Idol Passages in Second Isaiah," *Catholic Biblical Quarterly* 42 (1980): 450–64.

images'] place, attire and activities is inseparable from the belief that their temples are maps of the cosmos." Israel's high
priest, as a second Adam (Sir. 49:16–50:1 [Heb.]), takes over the
role of cult statue as "the visible and concrete image of the creator within the temple-as-microcosm."[34] In this vision of creation as a temple-palace, all "antechambers for lesser gods and
their statues have been emptied lest the sight of the creator God
in his human 'statue' in the central and highest holy of holies be
obscured."[35] Idolatry is therefore outlawed. It might also be that
Israel is to make no graven image since she is in fact sur-
rounded by God's "images": other human beings, marred though
they might be.

In this respect, the high priest standing in the Holy of Holies
models Israel's calling as Yahweh's holy nation-kingdom of
priests (Exod. 19:6) living in their holy sanctuary-land. On the
one hand, just as the Great King reigned in his cosmic temple-
palace in "Sabbath" rest, so his people incarnate this reality by
resting in their paradise-land, keeping the Sabbath day holy
(Exod. 20:8) and remembering the initial creation while at the
same time anticipating its restoration. On the other hand, as a
kingdom of priests, Israel too, by keeping Yahweh's commands
(i.e., daily repudiating Adam and Eve's rebellious autonomy)
and enjoying Yahweh's close personal presence, is to serve as
the bearer of Yahweh's image to the surrounding nations (Deut.
4:5–8). And what does this demonstrate if not the justice, righteousness, mercy, longsuffering kindness, and compassion that
characterize Yahweh himself?[36] Israel, as Yahweh's true son, is
utterly to reject the self-centered and ultimately murderous
way of Cain, Lamech, and those self-glorifying pretenders, the
sons of the gods. To be Yahweh's image-bearer means to look
like him, and nowhere is this more evident than in the Israelites' treatment, on the one hand, of one another, the sojourner,
and even the Egyptian, and on the other, of creation, including
the land and its animals. The former are to be shown the same

34. Fletcher-Louis, "God's Image," 8f.
35. Ibid., 3.
36. See, for example, Christopher H. Wright, *Living as the People of God*
(Leicester: Inter-Varsity, 1983).

mercy and care that Yahweh showered on Israel in the exodus,[37] and the latter are to enjoy their Sabbath rest as well.[38]

Idolatry, Loss of the Image, and Exile

Tragically, Israel, Yahweh's new humanity, rebels as did Adam and Eve. Yahweh's son forsakes him for idols. The problem is that since human beings bear the image of Yahweh, to worship an idol is to deny both Israel's identity in particular and humanity's in general. To seek to capture the essence of Yahweh in a lifeless image is not only impossible but also invites manipulation *of* him rather than a trusting and obedient relationship *with* him. And if people seek to manipulate an objectified deity, which is the essence of idolatry, it is no great revelation that they soon treat his image-bearers in like manner. Idolatry and injustice are correlatives, and the prophets fulminate against both.

Tragically, just as Pharaoh's idolatrously hardened heart led to the abuse of Israel, now the same hardness of heart in Israel's elites cause them to abuse the poor. The seriousness of this can be seen when bearing in mind the inherent logic of the cult-statue metaphor. The deity who was understood actually to indwell his image was to be honored by the provision of clothing, housing, and victuals. Consequently, to deprive at the very least one's fellow Israelites of such was to show utter contempt for Yahweh in whose image they were made. It is here that ethics and worship are inextricably bound. One cannot claim to worship Yahweh and then abuse the one thing made in his image: people (e.g., Isaiah 58; Jer. 7:1–29; Ezek. 18:5–18). It is not surprising then that the consequences of Israel's idolatry and oppression of the poor (Isaiah 5) are a judgment scene in Yahweh's temple (Isaiah 6) and the subsequent departure of Yahweh's

37. E.g., the requirement of care for the stranger (Exod. 23:9; Lev. 19:33–34; Deut. 10:17–19); of a rest day (Deut. 5:13–15); of justice and social concern for the weak (Deut. 24:17–18, 20–22); that Hebrew slaves should not be ruled over with cruelty (Lev. 25:43), are to be freed at Jubilee (Lev. 25:40), and must not go out empty-handed (Deut. 15:13–15); and even the command not to abhor the Egyptian (Deut. 23:7).
38. E.g., Exod. 23:12; Deut. 5:14–15; cf. Lev. 26:34–35, 43.

presence from his temple (Ezekiel 10), adumbrating Israel's own imminent departure from her sanctuary-land.

We earlier mentioned the Ezekiel passage in which Yahweh's formation of Israel and the formation of idols are connected. Given the humanity-as-God's-image metaphor, this is not surprising. The same connection is present in the commissioning of the prophet in Isaiah 6, fittingly situated in Yahweh's temple. (Remember its microcosmic and image symbolism.) Invoking what might be called the idolaters' curse of Psalms 115 and 135—those who worship idols become like them—idolatrous Israel is re-created in the image of the blind and deaf gods she worships: Having eyes, she will not see, ears, she will not hear (Isa. 6:9–10; cf. Deut. 4:28; Jer. 5:21; Ezek. 12:2).[39] Just as Adam and Eve in seeking autonomous wisdom found themselves naked and under sentence of death, expelled from the sanctuary garden, so too Israel, having rejected Yahweh's Word, will stagger naked (Deut. 28:48; Isa. 3:24; Ezek. 23:29; Hosea 2:3, 9; cf. Isa. 20:2–4; 47:2; Amos 2:16), imaging their lifeless idols even unto the death of exile (Ezek. 6:4; cf. Isa. 10:4; Jer. 7:33; 19:7–9; Lam. 2:20–21).

Given that image and creation are interconnected by means of the temple motif, we might expect creation also to be involved in the exile. It is perhaps not surprising then that the curse remains in effect until the land is made desolate (Isa. 6:11–12). It is interesting that the preceding chapter, immediately after Israel passes judgment on herself (5:1–4), lists six curses (5:8, 11, 18, 20, 21 [bis]), five of which directly concern her abuse of others, and concludes with the land having no light but only darkness in the midst of a roaring like the sea (5:30). This imagery, to my mind, echoes the chaos before creation, and the six curses of chapter 5 are an ironic echo of the six days of creation. This time, however, the word of Yahweh effects the dissolution of the good order of Israel's new Eden land. No longer superintended as it should be by Yahweh's image-bearers and simultaneously under a curse because of their rebellion, the land becomes a wasteland and a desert (Isa. 27:10; 32:12–14; 64:10; Jer. 4:23–26; 9:10–11; 22:6; Ezek. 19:10–14; Hosea 2:3; cf. Pss. 11:6; 68:6; Joel 2:3). Both sanctuary-land and image-bearer return to chaotic lifelessness.

39. Beale, "Isaiah vi 9–13: A Retributive Taunt against Idolatry," *Vetus Testamentum* 41 (1991): 257–78.

Promise of the Return

Yahweh, however, did not create the earth to be uninhabited (Isa. 45:18), and in keeping with the promise implied in his clothing of Adam and Eve, Israel, his new humanity, will yet be redeemed. Yahweh announces that in a new exodus he will bring salvation to his people (e.g., Isa. 45:8, 17; 46:13), restoring both them and their land and returning them to Jerusalem. This salvation in heart and body is characterized both by Israel's rejection of her idols (Isa. 2:20; 17:7–8; 27:9; 30:22; 31:7) and by Israel's turning to Yahweh, who alone gives sight and hearing (cf. Exod. 4:11; Ps. 146:5–9). The blind see, the deaf hear, the lame walk, and the dead are raised (Isa. 26:19; 35:5–6; 42:7, 16; Ezekiel 37). Echoing the creation of Adam and Eve, Israel is resurrected from the death of exile through word of divine utterance and the indwelling of Yahweh's Spirit (Ezek. 37:5–6, 14) to become the true bearer of his image (Isa. 32:15; 44:3; 59:21). No longer bearing the likeness of her lifeless, blind, deaf, mute, and stony-hearted idols, Israel now lives, sees, hears, speaks, and has a heart of flesh (Ezek. 11:19). Fully clothed, arrayed with the glorious garments of righteousness, and anointed with the oil of rejoicing, she finds rest in her restored sanctuary-land (Ps. 132:9, 16, 18; Isa. 23:18; 52:1; 61:10; Zech. 3:3–5; 14:14).

The new Adam/humanity motif inherent in the hope of the return is central to Daniel 7. Reminiscent of Genesis 1:2, the prophet's vision opens with darkness and a wind-swept stormy sea (Dan. 7:2). It soon becomes clear, however, that this is a demonic anti-creation scene, since what emerges is not the goodness of Yahweh's well-ordered cosmos but increasingly horrendous, violent, and mutant beasts, symbolizing human attempts to create themselves and the world in their own image (cf. the parallel vision in Daniel 2). For a time these beasts oppress the saints, but then over against them "one in human form," a truly human being, appears. This "son of man," whether true Israel and/or Israel's messianic representative, a true bearer of the image, will subdue the beasts as did Adam before him.[40]

40. N. T. Wright, *The New Testament and the People of God* (Minneapolis: Fortress, 1992), 267, 91–96.

Not surprisingly, this new exodus/new creation of the image is also accompanied by a re-creation of the land. Carol Stuhlmueller has noted the integration of exodus and creation imagery in Isaiah.[41] The close link between these two events is evident in several passages in which restoration of the image is immediately followed by that of creation. Thus, Isaiah 35:5–6 (NRSV):

> Then the eyes of the blind shall be opened,
>   and the ears of the deaf unstopped;
> then the lame shall leap like a deer,
>   and the tongue of the speechless sing for joy.
> For waters shall break forth in the wilderness,
>   and streams in the desert;
> the burning sand shall become a pool,
>   and the thirsty ground springs of water.

So too Isaiah 32:15: "until a spirit from on high is poured out on us, and the wilderness becomes a fruitful field, and the fruitful field is deemed a forest" (NRSV). Likewise, Ezekiel's vision of a resurrected and reconstituted Israel (Ezekiel 37) is followed by his vision of a restored temple and a re-created land whose swarming creatures of earth and sea recall the language of Genesis 1 (vv. 11–12, 21–25; cf. Ezek. 47:7–10). The land is to be a new Eden (Isa. 51:3; Ezek. 36:35; Joel 2:3; cf. Isa. 65:21–23 LXX).

Finally, this was never a matter just for Israel. From the very beginning, Abraham's children were called to be a source of blessing to the nations. Nowhere is this more apparent than in Isaiah's great hope of restored Israel being a light to the nations (Isa. 2:1–5; 19:22–25; 42:1–7; 49:6). Yahweh intends that the nations, even those at the ends of the earth, will also be restored and will enjoy the world he created to be not empty but inhabited (Isa. 45:18, 22).

In spite of these great promises, however, it becomes evident that they had not materialized. Some people had returned to the land, but the full hopes of restoration had not materialized.[42]

41. *Creative Redemption in Deutero-Isaiah,* Analecta biblica 43 (Rome: Pontifical Biblical Institute, 1970); and idem, "The Theology of Creation in Second Isaias," *Catholic Biblical Quarterly* 21 (1959): 429–67.

42. On the delay of the new exodus, see Wright, *New Testament,* 268–71; Craig A. Evans, "Jesus and the Continuing Exile of Israel," in *Jesus and the Restoration of Israel,* ed. Carey C. Newman (Downers Grove, Ill.: InterVarsity; Carlisle, U.K.: Paternoster, 1999), 77–100.

Jesus and Restoration of the Image

It is now increasingly recognized among New Testament scholars that Jesus cannot properly be understood apart from Israel's restorationist hopes. That is to say that Jesus is the one who inaugurates Israel's new exodus/new creation return from exile, particularly as expressed in the scroll of Isaiah. Picked up especially in Mark,[43] this idea is also echoed in Matthew and Luke, even if elaborated on according to their own theological agendas.[44] John's account of the life of Jesus also begins with allusions to creation—"in the beginning was the Word"—and the exodus—"the Word became flesh and lived among us, and we have seen his glory . . . full of grace and truth" (1:1, 14 NRSV).

Not only does Jesus' story begin with John the Baptist's preaching of Isaiah's proclamation of deliverance (Isa. 40:3),[45] but Jesus' baptism and temptation recapitulate Israel's exodus experience of being declared God's son, passing through the waters, and facing temptation in the desert.[46] This time, however, Yahweh's Son, indwelt by his Spirit, remains faithful to his image-bearing calling. This Son of man, this truly human one, does only what he sees the Father doing (John 5:15–23; 11:38; 14:8–11). Jesus' preaching (Isa. 61:1–2 in Luke 4), healings (Isaiah 35, 61 in Matt. 11:2–6; par. Luke 7:18–23), and exorcisms (Isa. 49:24 in Mark 3:22–27) announce and inaugurate Israel's long-awaited new exodus/new creational restoration. The feedings in the desert and Jesus' power over the sea likewise recall the exodus and, along with the marvelous provision of wine (Joel 3:18; Amos 9:13) and abundant catches of fish (Ezek. 47:9–10), testify to the new creational activity of Yahweh among his people.[47] Not surprisingly, the evangelists' terminol-

---

43. Rikk E. Watts, *Isaiah's New Exodus and Mark* (Grand Rapids: Baker, 2000).

44. See, for example, Dale C. Allison, *The New Moses: A Matthean Typology* (Minneapolis: Fortress, 1993); and David W. Pao, *Acts and the Isaianic New Exodus*, Wissenschaftliche Untersuchungen zum Neuen Testament 2:130 (Tübingen: Mohr [Paul-Siebeck], 2000).

45. See Watts, *Isaiah's New Exodus*, 82–84, for a survey of the many citations of and allusions to this passage in the context of Israel's future hope.

46. Ibid., 102–18.

47. See Rikk E. Watts, *Jesus and the Mighty Deeds of Yahweh*, forthcoming from Baker.

ogy of "mighty deeds," "signs," and "works" deliberately echoes
the exodus (Deut. 3:24; 4:34; Pss. 44:1–3; 106:8) and creation
(Pss. 65:6; 107:24).

As in the first exodus, Israel is called to repudiate Adam
and Eve's image-defiling autonomy. Jesus' teaching a new
Torah (Matthew 5–7; notably followed by ten mighty deeds—
a blessed reversal of the ten plagues?)[48] and his choosing of
twelve disciples are nothing less than a reconstitution of Israel in the image of Yahweh. But instead of the grace of
Torah there has come a greater grace and truth (John 1:17;
cf. Psalm 119). What is it? Surely it is his self-giving for us
(Isaiah 53; Mark 10:45),[49] but it is also his declaration that
loving God is not so much about Sabbath-keeping as it is
about people-keeping (Mark 2:27). True, Sabbath rest matters, but people matter more. Why? Because although the
law is good and spiritual (cf. Rom. 7:12, 14), it is not made in
God's image; only people are. Consequently, Jesus teaches
his disciples how to walk in Yahweh's ways, giving them a
heart of flesh by leading his blind disciples "along a path they
do not know," namely, the way of cross-bearing servanthood
(Isa. 42:16; so Mark 8:14–10:52).[50] Here then is the replacement of the idolatrously stony hard heart. No longer infected
by the heart-hardening idolatrous leaven of Herod and the
Pharisees, reconstituted Israel is again summoned to live out
the compassion of Yahweh.[51] Thus, while individuals are summoned, they are summoned to a community of cruciform existence in which true holiness is intrinsically related to how

48. Allison, *New Moses*, 207–13.

49. Although the influence of Isaiah 53 on Mark 10:45 has been debated, see
now Rikk E. Watts, "Jesus' Death, Isaiah 53, and Mark 10:45: A Crux Revisit-
ed," in *Jesus the Suffering Servant: Isaiah 53 and Christian Origins*, ed.
William H. Bellinger, Jr., and William R. Farmer (Harrisburg, Pa.: Trinity,
1998), 125–51.

50. Watts, *Isaiah's New Exodus*, 239–57.

51. It was Yahweh's compassion that undergirded the promises of the new
exodus (e.g., Isa. 49:10, 13, 15; 54:8, 10; 55:7; cf. Deut. 4:31; 30:3; 32:6; Pss.
111:4; 112:4; 145:8). It is likely not unintentional that the only individuals
showing compassion in the Gospels are Jesus (Matt. 9:36; 14:14; 15:32; 20:34;
Mark 1:41; 6:34; 8:2; Luke 7:13) and those who act like God (Matt. 18:27; Luke
10:33; 15:20).

they treat even the little ones who follow Jesus (Mark 9:33–10:45).[52]

But this is not merely a matter of the heart. Reflecting the compassion of Yahweh, Jesus also sets right the image through the healing of the blind, deaf, lame, and mute and ultimately through the resurrection of the dead. If the whole person is integral to bearing Yahweh's image, then the whole person must be restored. Jesus, therefore, restores the sight of blind Bartimaeus, son of uncleanness, leading him back into Jerusalem (Mark 10:46–52), and the blind and lame who come to him find healing in the temple (Matt. 21:14). Physical healing is integral to this salvific restoration.

Here then we see the locus of Jesus' deity and humanity. Because he is in some mysterious way God himself among us,[53] he can, through the indwelling Spirit, perfectly reflect the image of God. As the Son of man, he can not only deliver and restore us but also show us what it means to be truly human. And because the God who is God of the living, not the dead, is faithful, Jesus' resurrection announces the ultimate destination of all those who faithfully learn from him what it means to look like the God in whose image they were made.

Finally, in keeping with the image-spirit connection, this true image-bearer in whom the Spirit dwelt would also be the one through whom the Spirit would be outpoured (Mark 1:7–8; par. Matt. 3:11–12; Luke 3:15–16). For John it is this Spirit, who constitutes the presence of Jesus when Jesus himself is absent, who will speak for and of Jesus in leading us into all truth and wisdom (John 14:15–27; 16:5–15; 20:22).

Space and time limitations preclude anything but a cursory examination of the rest of the New Testament.[54] Jesus is plainly declared to be the genuine image of the invisible God (2 Cor. 4:4; Col. 1:15), a new Adam (Rom. 5:12–19; 1 Cor. 15:21–22, 45–49), and

52. I have not cited Matt. 25:31–46 here since this concerns how the faithful followers of Jesus are treated by the nations (cf. Matt. 12:48–50), which in itself reaffirms that those who follow Jesus and are filled with his Spirit are intended to be his image-bearers (Matt. 10:40–42).

53. As much of Wright's *Jesus and the Victory of God* implies, Jesus in so many ways acts like Yahweh himself is present in him.

54. On the centrality of new creation in the New Testament, see Beale, "Eschatological Conception."

the beginning of a new humanity, the firstborn of the new creation (Col. 1:15, 18). In every respect, he is qualified, as Hebrews declares, to be our true High Priest (Heb. 4:14–8:13) and so to lead us into our ultimate Sabbath rest (Heb. 4:1–11). In Christ, the beginning of the new creation, God has declared, "Let light shine out of darkness" (2 Cor. 4:6 NRSV), whereby we are "transformed into the same image from one degree of glory to another" (2 Cor. 3:18 NRSV),[55] having the same mind that was in Christ Jesus (Phil. 2:1–18). The glory of the image of God, now revealed in the mystery of the Trinity, is to be found in face-to-face beholding of and fellowship with the Father through the crucified Son, whose presence is now mediated by the Spirit. Granted, the Trinity is a mystery. But perhaps that is the very point. Being human—male and female—is itself a deep mystery. No longer naked and defiled, the image-bearer is clothed with a glorious righteousness.

As with the ancient formation of cult images, reception of the Spirit is crucial to Christian existence.[56] Through his presence he stamps the *telos* of the law on our hearts, marking us as God's new creational "sons" (Rom. 8:12–17; 1 Cor. 2:6–16; Gal. 3:1–5, 14; 4:6; 5:16) and thus as his holy kingdom of priests (1 Peter 2:4–5). The central fact of the Christian's life is that he or she is a new creature (2 Cor. 5:17; Gal. 6:15), filled with the Spirit, sharing in Christ's suffering, and imitating Yahweh in terms of fruits and gifts (1 Corinthians 12–14; Gal. 5:16–26).[57] As with Jesus, this includes the promised healing of the body in the present and the future (1 Cor. 12:9; James 5:14–18).

Whereas the Holy of Holies in the Jerusalem temple was the original locus of the presence, we are now, collectively and individually, the temple of the Holy Spirit. We are "in Christ," reigning with him in the heavenlies (Eph. 1:18–23; 2:6), joined to one another and to him, created to do good works (Eph. 2:10), reflecting his character (Ephesians 4–6) and therefore partaking of the new Adam (Romans 5). We are the true Israel

55. On the exodus background to this text, see S. J. Hafemann, *Paul, Moses, and the History of Israel,* Wissenschaftliche Untersuchungen zum Neuen Testament 81 (Tübingen: Mohr [Paul-Siebeck], 1995).

56. See Gordon D. Fee, *Paul, the Spirit, and the People of God* (Peabody, Mass.: Hendrickson, 1996).

57. On suffering and the Spirit, see Scott J. Hafemann, *Suffering and Ministry in the Spirit* (Grand Rapids: Eerdmans, 1990).

(Gal. 6:15–16) and thus the true image of God (Eph. 4:1–5; Phil. 2:1–16). Again this is not merely an individual relationship. What we see, as the vision of Ephesians makes clear, is the re-formation of all humanity into the one people of God, such that there is "no longer Jew or Greek, there is no longer slave or free, there is no longer male and female" (Gal. 3:28 NRSV)—perhaps the most radical words uttered by a human being in the first century and even beyond. Of course, the other side to this is that those who refuse to acknowledge God in the end lose touch with their own embodied humanity, even distorting the gift of being able to work with God in creating and filling the creation with other bearers of his image (Romans 1).

But what about the creation? Neither Jesus nor Paul seems to concern himself overmuch with the cosmos as temple-palace. Yet this does not indicate a marginalization of the cosmos. The restoration of humanity as the bearer of God's image, which they emphasize, is the key to creation's restoration. As already noted, the fate of creation is linked to that of the image-bearer. It is pre-pared as a habitation for humanity and suffers when humans rebel, both at the cosmic level of the universe, which comes under a curse, and the microcosmic level of Israel and her land. When Israel rebels, her land and Yahweh's house are laid waste. When she is restored, the land lives and the temple is rebuilt.

Consequently, while there is evidence of the restoration of the fecundity and flourishing of creation at Jesus' behest (as is evident in the turning of water into wine, the multiplication of the loaves, and the abundance of fish), this concern for human-ity indicates that the key issue is the restoration of the image-bearer. Creation's fate, as temple-palace for the image-bearer, is intimately linked to the authenticity of the image-bearer. Therefore, Paul can say that just as our rebellion caused cre-ation to be subjected to the futility of not achieving its intended goal, so "creation waits with eager longing for the revealing of the children of God; . . . in hope that the creation itself will be set free from its bondage to decay and will obtain the freedom of the glory of the children of God" (Rom. 8:19–21 NRSV).[58] For

58. E.g., C. E. B. Cranfield, "Some Observations on Romans 8:19–21," in *Reconciliation and Hope: The Leon Morris Festschrift*, ed. R. Banks (Exeter: Paternoster, 1974).

those who long for the restoration of creation, the biblical answer is: become a true son or daughter of God. In the present,
imitate him by caring for and tending the creation while awaiting its final redemption.

The ultimate goal, therefore, is the merging of heaven and
earth. John's final vision is of the descent of the New Jerusalem
so that the dwelling of God might be with humanity (Rev. 21:2–
5, 15–27). Several aspects are worth noting. There is no temple
in this massive cube-shaped city (Rev. 21:22). The fact that the
only other such shapes are the Holy of Holies in the tabernacle
and Solomon's temple[59] suggests that the city itself has become
not just the temple but the very Holy of Holies (cf. also Ezek.
45:2–3). Furthermore, the astounding dimensions—12,000 sta-
dia (approximately 1,500 miles) along each axis—correspond
to those of the then-known Greek world,[60] indicating that the
climax of the new creation is not the abandonment of the earth
but the coming of Yahweh to the earth to dwell among us. This,
then, is the climax of Genesis 1's sixfold affirmation of the
goodness of creation with its progression from heaven to earth.
The final goal is not the destruction of creation but rather the
unification of heaven and earth such that the renewed earth itself becomes Yahweh's throne room. We are not going to
heaven. Heaven is coming here.

But the process is not yet complete, since this salvation, this
new exodus/new creational restoration of the image and subsequently creation, is still taking place. We are indeed saved
(Rom. 8:15–17; Eph. 2:5, 8), but we are also being saved (1 Cor.
1:18) and shall yet be saved (Rom. 5:9–11). The key in between
the times is for us to live the life of the Spirit and so again be
true bearers of the image and thus Yahweh's agents of new creation (Eph. 5:10–20; cf. Isa. 59:15b–21; 63:1–6).

This image-temple-palace paradigm may also give some insight into Old and New Testament ethics, for surely to be saved,
as James and Paul both well understood, means to reflect God's
character. In a recent discussion with language professor David

59. See 1 Kings 6:20; 2 Chron. 3:8; cf. the Holy Place in Ezekiel's temple,
500 cubits square, Ezek. 42:16–20; 45:2.
60. See G. K. Beale, *The Book of Revelation,* New International Greek Testament Commentary (Grand Rapids: Eerdmans, 1999), 1073–74.

Clemens, he noted that, whether because of Socratic scholasticism or an aversion to anything that smacks of Roman Catholicism, the study of Old Testament ritual is an area that has long languished in the exile of critical Protestant scholarship. But things have changed. Ritual criticism—the comparative study of the role of ritual in the ancient world, on which this paper in part relies—is now a burgeoning field. Ritual, it is now recognized, serves an important role in concretizing doctrine. The priests of the ancient world and the people whom they represented were heavily engaged in ritual formation and animation and in sustaining the image of the god in its temple-palace. Israel too engaged in ritual to incarnate what might otherwise have become merely abstract theological ideas. Interestingly, there is little ritual in the New Testament. What if, given the understanding of what it means to be human and that we are indwelt by the presence of the Spirit, New Testament ethics is the counterpart of Old Testament ritual? That is, our concretizing of theology is seen not so much in aspects of religious cultic observance as in our care for one another. As Jesus declared, the whole law is summed up in two commands: to love God and to love one's neighbor (Mark 12:28–34; cf. Matt. 7:12).

Implications

Whereto from here? For Homer, salvation was in part the affirmation of the self through heroic action (one recalls *Gladiator*'s "What we do in life echoes in eternity"), even if this meant the abandonment of wife and family. Eventually, having made one's mark, one could return—though perhaps for too many Ulysses the return has been too late to save either wife or child from the chaos resulting from the absent father or, now in modern times, the absent mother. For the Stoics, the *logos* represented that order of the rational, the good, and the beautiful, evident to varying degrees in the creation, including both humans and the world. Salvation consisted of conforming the human *psychē*, encased as it was in the *sōma*, to the harmonious stasis of the *logos*. This was achieved positively by adhering to "natural" instinct and negatively by subduing, negating, or avoiding the chaotic, whether internal or external. Eventually, whether at death or the final cataclysm, the fiery *logos* would be reunited with itself before being scattered in an act of new creation to begin the cycle all over again. Such a salvation resulted in this life in an essentially individualistic existence, with the Stoic virtues amounting to self-discipline, such that the *pyschē*'s instinctive conformity to the *logos* of nature was not disturbed, whether internally through uncontrolled passions or externally through the discordant actions of other persons or events. Love of others did not motivate but rather a concern for the self. This remained so even though Stoicism entailed taking care of others, since, by virtue of the interrelatedness of nature via the indwelling *logos*, to care for others meant finally to do good to oneself.

The Gnostics went further. For them the material world was an unauthorized and monstrous creation of a foolish lower god aided by even lower and clumsy archons who sought to manipulate humanity according to their purposes. Only through enlightenment by *gnōsis* could the souls or *pneuma* of a special cadre of elite and chosen human beings escape the material world. The final resolution would occur with the dissolution of the physical creation and the reunification of enlightened and now liberated spirits with the absolute "Unknown god" in the kingdom of light. According to this view, only some human beings were worthy and the present world denigrated.

The Renaissance was occasioned in part by the rediscovery of the Stoic vision of nature and the Homeric view of the hero. The created world began to be considered on its own terms, its own beauty and rationality. Whether through the art of Leonardo da Vinci, the Portuguese explorers and their practical goal of incremental navigation, or Machiavelli's pragmatism in the realm of political theory, the regnant theological view of creation was gradually marginalized.

As this movement flowered, salvation slowly became a matter of human mastery of creation through humanity's own powers of observation and reason. Standing between Galileo and Newton, Descartes' "I doubt therefore I am" can perhaps, in the terms of this discussion, be seen as a modified recapitulation of Gnosticism with a touch of the heroic. First, the *logos* was largely reduced to pure reason. Second, creation, while not seen as evil, was nevertheless neutralized, such that within a century and a half the cosmos was no longer described as "creation" but as "nature." As such it was simply "out there" and subject to human manipulation in whatever ways humanity chose. Thus, as in Gnosticism, there was an alienation from nature, with reason emulating the Gnostics' *pneuma*, enlightenment being the liberation of reason from the shackles of tradition, and humanity's relationship to the world being reduced merely to that of power exercised, à la Francis Bacon, through the subversive discovery of nature's laws. Third, in positing each enlightened individual as an objective observer viewing nature with the god's-eye view of human reason, the project of salvation through knowledge took on the character of an individualistic heroic enterprise, and with it came a consequent alienation from one another.

It was against this denigration of nature and human sensuality, by confining value solely to the realm of reason, that Friedrich Nietzsche rebelled. Lauding Jesus but excoriating Paul, whom he held, mistakenly, at least partly responsible for Christianity's corruption, Nietzsche raged against the otherworldly and body-quelling bent of the church. Rejecting the elaborate and intellectually sterile Socratic argumentation of the Western academy, Nietzsche elected to employ Cynic aphorism, which he felt was far more human. Salvation, if there was any, was to be found in the here and now in the authentic human existence (in the technical sense of the Greek, αὐθέντης, to be an autocrat, absolute master).

Ironically, as the twentieth century's growing disillusionment with science has indicated, far from returning us to the light, our exercise of reason has led us instead to become more like the clumsy archons, threatening our very existence on this planet. On the other hand, as Jim Houston has argued, the rise of the modern therapeutic recapitulates the central affirmation of both the Stoic and the Gnostic that we are at our core good and that it is only the external chaos that prevents our perfection. For many moderns, the fault lies outside, not within. Salvation is to be found in liberation from debilitating externals, whether others' demands or even one's own body, and in the unfettered expression of the Bohemian "free spirit." But ironically, those who appear to have the most freedom seem to be the most enslaved, and Nietzsche's authentic human existence seems only to have resulted in, not unlike his own experience, increased alienation.

It seems that nearly every modern attempt at salvation is a kind of recapitulation of these historic and ancient errors. To such there is a clear Christian response: The problem is not creation, nor is it external to us, nor is its answer to be found within us, whether individually or collectively. It is located in the heart of the image-bearer.

Thus, while creation needs to be subdued—in keeping with the good character and creativity of Yahweh—it is not inherently the enemy. It is good. As the Stoics recognized, the good, the beautiful, and the ordered can also be seen in the handiwork of God. Nor is it merely to be discarded, since it is destined for salvation. After all, the New Jerusalem descends to earth. Counter to both the Stoics and the Gnostics, whether ancient or modern, salvation is not to be found in escape from the earth. Nietzsche was on to something. But neither, contrary to the thinking of Nietzsche and some radical environmentalists, is salvation to be found in a heroic acceptance of our humanity or in a symbiotic relationship to the earth. Rather, salvation is intimately connected with the image-bearer imitating the God who created the world by being incarnated, as he was, in it. It is not a flight from but a commitment to take our gardening role seriously, not an escape but a commitment to a new creational gardening of the earth.

As with creation, so too with our humanity. It is not to be run from or split into the all-important mind and insignificant if not burdensome body. We bear the image in our complete humanity—hearts-minds, embodied form—and this must not be forgotten in the interplay of the individual and the collective, of the male and the female. The biblical account envisages not only the indwelling Spirit and knowledge of God but also fully active bodies and the sensual pleasures of feasting and drinking.

But eating and drinking are best done together. And so this salvation is not to be found in the Homeric hero who in pursuit of his own distinction abandons his wife and child, or in the Stoic attempt to order one's personal life in keeping with the *logos* of the cosmos, or in the Cynic personal rebellion against stultifying social mores. We must first admit that creation is too wonderful for us. Its mysteries require humility, not self-authenticating heroics. Second, we are made for the other, and without the other we are not complete.

The wisdom that will heal our sorrows and end our exile is not that of better technical control. To use John's terms, we need the one from above, the only one who has seen the Father, who speaks his words, and who demonstrates his love for his abundant creation, if we are to become truly the image-bearers that this earth was designed for and for whose revelation it so desperately longs. The best eating and drinking is doing the will of the Father—namely, to learn from Christ, to cast in our lot with his happy band. As image-bearers we will know *shalom* only when we submit to the one in whose image we were made.

It seems incumbent on us, therefore, to ensure that we are saved, that we are being saved, and that we are anticipating that day when we will be saved. Only thus can our incarnation of this good and great salvation be faithful in its totality as we work with God in the restoration of the image-bearer, body and soul, and thus too in the restoration of creation.

2

"Let Us See Thy Great Salvation"

What Did It Mean to Be Saved for the Early Evangelicals?

D. BRUCE HINDMARSH

Is the typical evangelical understanding of salvation too narrow? Are evangelicals preoccupied with mere "soul saving," and do they regard social concerns as secondary to or even a distraction from the gospel? Anxiety about these questions was present when evangelicals from around the world gathered in 1974 at Lausanne, Switzerland, for a congress on global evangelization. The question they hoped to answer was, What is the relationship between social action and evangelism? John Stott was instrumental at that gathering in helping evangelicals unite social concern and evangelism under the rubric of mission. The Lausanne Covenant included the statement: "The salvation we claim should be transforming us in the totality of our personal and social responsibilities."[1] Again, these concerns were united in the Manila Manifesto of 1989, a document of the Lausanne Committee for World Evangelization. The unifying principle was identified as the kingdom of God, since the kingdom must be proclaimed by word and deed: "As we preach the Kingdom of God we must be committed to its demands of justice and peace."[2]

The anxieties felt at the Lausanne meetings concerning the relationship between evangelism and social concern can be traced back to the so-called great reversal of the early twentieth century, when many conservative evangelicals in the English-speaking world repudiated their earlier engagement with social issues, in part as a reaction to the rise of the liberal social gospel, associated in America with theologians such as Walter Rauschenbusch.[3] By the time of the First World War, conservative evangelicals had become highly suspicious of any Christian social agenda, because such agendas seemed increasingly linked with theological liberalism and seemed to supplant evangelism. John Horsch, for example, worried that the social gospel taught that education and sanitation should take the place of regeneration and the work of the Holy Spirit.[4] Others appealed to history and argued that evangelicals had always been wary of devotional energy being siphoned off into social reform. The *Methodist Recorder* in 1912 claimed, "Our fathers were much more concerned about the glory of God and the dishonour done to him than about any social prob-

---

1. Oliver Barclay, *Evangelicalism in Britain, 1935–1995* (Leicester: Inter-Varsity, 1997), 110. There was debate at Lausanne about whether all acts for the good of society should be taken as a manifestation of the kingdom or whether the term *kingdom* should be reserved for the actions of believers. The consensus (though there was a supplementary paper) was that the latter view was the more biblical one (111).

2. John R. W. Stott, *Making Christ Known: Historic Mission Documents from the Lausanne Movement, 1974–1989* (Grand Rapids: Eerdmans, 1997). See also Robert T. Coote and John R. W. Stott, *Down to Earth: Studies in Christianity and Culture: The Papers of the Lausanne Consultation on Gospel and Culture* (Grand Rapids: Eerdmans, 1980).

3. See David Bebbington, *Evangelicalism in Modern Britain* (London: Unwin Hyman, 1989), 214–17; and George Marsden, *Fundamentalism and American Culture* (New York: Oxford University Press, 1980), 85–93.

4. Marsden, *Fundamentalism and American Culture*, 255.

lems."[5] The Lausanne documents of 1974 and 1989 addressed this widespread suspicion on the part of evangelicals that Christian social engagement might somehow compromise the gospel.

Perhaps there is a congenital weakness in the evangelical tradition that pulls evangelicals in the direction of withdrawal from society and a privatized, individualistic piety. If so, there has, however, also been a recurring countervailing impulse to engage and reform society and to express faith in public works. The causes of abolition and temperance remain the two classic examples of nineteenth-century evangelical social and political involvement. The Lausanne discussions, along with a host of political, cultural, and charitable initiatives begun by evangelicals in the second half of the twentieth century, witness to a significant effort to redress the effects of the great reversal and restore a more balanced evangelical integration of gospel proclamation and social concern.

The essays in this book each respond in their own way to the question of what it means to be saved and whether the evangelical understanding of salvation has anything to say in regard to contemporary concerns about race (Bacote), class (Sherman), and gender (Nordling), or whether an evangelical theology of sin and atonement (Blocher), the image of God (Watts), and creation (Wilkinson) can contribute to the biblical concern for a comprehensive salvation. It may be helpful to see this present work about salvation as a continuation of the conversation among evangelicals during the past century: What does salvation include, and what does it imply?

This essay draws on the early history of evangelicalism to provide an example of the sort of integrated proclamation of the gospel by word and deed called for by Lausanne. As we reflect on evangelical soteriology, it is important that we not have a foreshortened perspective, for if our historical memory reaches back no farther than to the era of fundamentalism and the great reversal or perhaps to the domestic piety and urban revivalism during the gilded age of Dwight L. Moody and Ira Sankey, then we will fail to recognize the resources within evangelicalism for its own renewal. We need to probe further if we wish to find more robust models of the integration of evangelism and broader concerns.

5. Quoted in Bebbington, *Evangelicalism in Modern Britain*, 215.

46   **Basic Reconsiderations**

There are many models we could examine, such as the social reformers William Wilberforce or Lord Shaftesbury in the nineteenth
century, but I would like to observe how the Good News of God's
salvation was announced at the outset of the evangelical movement
in the eighteenth century. The early evangelicals preached a message of salvation from sin through personal faith in Christ as the
only hope of eternal life and the only way to avoid eternal damna-
tion because they believed this is what the Bible teaches. Nevertheless, their typical concerns were much broader than merely
getting souls saved and on their way to heaven.

I would like to begin, therefore, in 1738, the year that John Wesley went to a meeting on Aldersgate Street in London and heard
someone reading from Martin Luther's preface to *The Epistle to
the Romans*. "About a quarter before nine in the evening," says
Wesley, "while he was describing the change which God works in
the heart through faith in Christ, I felt my heart strangely warmed.
I felt I did trust in Christ, Christ alone for salvation; and an assurance was given me that He had taken away *my* sins, even *mine*,
and saved *me* from the law of sin and death."[6]

This statement from Wesley's biography reveals a number of key
and enduring elements in the evangelical conception of salvation,
such as the influence of Luther and the Reformation as a theological heritage, the stress on the heart and simple direct trust in Christ,
the sense of deliverance from both sin and death, and an emphasis
on the individual, as evidenced by the string of first-person personal
pronouns (me, my, mine). This statement has been at the center of
one of the longest debates in Wesleyan studies about the role of this
Aldersgate experience in Wesley's formation and theology, but it
suffices for now as a symbol of salvation within evangelicalism.[7]

6. John Wesley, May 24, 1738, *Journals and Diaries I (1735–38)*, ed.
W. Reginald Ward and Richard P. Heitzenrater, vol. 18 of *The Bicentennial
Edition of the Works of John Wesley* (Nashville: Abingdon, 1976–), 249–50. (All
references to Wesley's *Works* in the notes below are to this edition, unless otherwise indicated.)

7. On the debates surrounding Aldersgate, see Randy L. Maddox, ed.,
Aldersgate Reconsidered (Nashville: Kingswood Books, Abingdon, 1990); idem,
"Celebrating Wesley—When?" *Methodist History* 29 (1991): 63–75; Kenneth J.
Collins, "Other Thoughts on Aldersgate: Has the Conversionist Paradigm Col-
lapsed?" *Methodist History* 30 (1991): 10–25; Randy L. Maddox, "Continuing
the Conversation," *Methodist History* 30 (1992): 235–41; and the collection of
articles in *Wesleyan Theological Journal* 24 (1989): 7–73.

On first reading, though, the statement intensifies the question of whether this early evangelical understanding of salvation is enough. Is Wesley unduly individualistic with all this language of *me* and *mine?* Is his reading of Luther on justification unduly narrow, legal, and again individualistic? Finally, is his stress on feelings and the heart a good deal too "pietistic," in the sense of being private, sentimental, and removed from a larger sense of the salvation of human society and the renewal of the world?

We can add a sharper edge to these questions by linking Wesley's experience of salvation to the Enlightenment. David Bebbington, one of the leading historians of the evangelical movement, has argued in stark terms: "The Evangelical version of Protestantism was created by the Enlightenment."[8] In our contemporary situation, a number of critics have analyzed modernity and concluded that the Enlightenment, with its conception of human autonomy, was the beginning of our troubles. It represented the rise of individualism and a pathological naïveté about the interconnectedness of self and society. So our sharpened question might be to ask whether evangelicalism, emerging as it did in the *Zeitgeist* of the Enlightenment, narrowed the concept of salvation, limiting it to the individual and thereby sacrificing its larger biblical sense.

Having set the case in such stark terms, it might come as a surprise to discover how widely the concerns of many early evangelicals extended in their efforts to announce the Good News to their generation. The discussion that follows examines the life and thought of John Wesley (1703–91) and identifies five concerns evident in his evangelistic ministry that are significantly broader than soul saving. These concerns are the poor, the body, society, the wider church, and the full and final salvation of the believer. I have chosen to deal principally with Wesley because he is a major figure as a theologian and a widely influential man of action. His considerable oeuvre, therefore, reveals not only what he said but also how he embodied these ideals in his ministry. A few other figures appear along the way, but Wesley's case is sufficient to illustrate that several concerns animated eighteenth-century evangelicals when they proclaimed the gospel.

8. Bebbington, *Evangelicalism in Modern Britain*, 74.

Good News for the Poor

The first point to note, then, is that Wesley did not simply
announce Good News; he announced Good News to the poor.
Wesley understood his mission as having a particular focus on
the poor, whom he believed had a privileged place in God's
program. As his brother Charles wrote:

> He speaks,—and, listening to his voice,
>   New life the dead receive;
> The mournful, broken hearts rejoice;
> The humble poor believe.[9]

In his apologetic work, *A Farther Appeal to Men of Reason
and Religion* (1745), Wesley wrote:

> The rich, the honorable, the great, we are thoroughly willing . . .
> to leave to you. Only let us alone with the poor, the vulgar, the
> base, the outcasts of men. Take also to yourselves the saints of
> the world: But suffer us "to call sinners to repentance"; even the
> most vile, the most ignorant, the most abandoned, the most
> fierce and savage of whom we can hear.[10]

Again, he declared simply, "I love the poor; in many of them I
find pure, serious grace, unmixed with paint, folly and affecta-
tion."[11] Two decades later, after countless miles of itinerancy,
Wesley remarked in passing that he had caught "the itch" a
hundred times by his close contact with the poor in his travels,
sharing their beds and shaking their hands.[12]
Wesley understood the sense in which the poor, the lowly,
and the humble were closer to the kingdom of God than were
the rich, since they were not so easily impeded by self-righ-

9. Charles Wesley, "O for a Thousand Tongues," in John and Charles Wesley, *A Collection of Hymns for the Use of the People Called Methodists* (London:
Wesleyan Conference Office, 1877), 5.
10. John Wesley, *Works*, 3d ed., vol. 3, ed. Thomas Jackson (London, 1872),
239.
11. Quoted in Henry Rack, *Reasonable Enthusiast* (London: Epworth,
1989), 363.
12. John Walsh, *John Wesley 1703–1791: A Bicentennial Tribute*, Friends of
Dr. Williams's Library Forty-Eighth Lecture (London: Friends of Dr. Williams's Library, 1993), 13.

teousness. They were more readily disposed to acknowledge their destitution and naked dependence on God's mercy. Moreover, Wesley maintained a sociology of mission that understood that the gospel went to work on a society normally from the bottom up, not the top down:

> And in every nation under heaven we may reasonably believe God will observe the same order which he hath done from the beginning of Christianity. "They shall all know *me*," saith the Lord, not from the greatest to the least . . . but, "from the least to the greatest."[13]

Wesley continued, "Before the end, *even* the rich shall enter into the kingdom of God" (emphasis added) and with them the powerful. The very last to enter the kingdom, according to Wesley, will be the academics: "Last of all the wise and learned, the men of genius, the philosophers, will be convinced that they are fools; will be 'converted, and become as little children, and enter into the kingdom of God.'"[14]

In numerous other ways we can observe Wesley's special concern for the poor, the marginalized, and the outsider. While his contemporary George Whitefield loved to play to the large crowds at Moorfields or the Boston Common or to engage in fashionable *salon* evangelism for the Countess of Huntingdon, Wesley typically spent his time with small groups of poor people, the forlorn and forsaken in outlying towns and villages or the new urban poor on the outskirts of London, Bristol, and Newcastle. He also engaged in many practical programs such as circulating libraries, medical dispensaries, schools for the poor, and housing for widows. When unemployment was high in 1741, he urged Methodists in London to donate clothes and to make a weekly gift of a penny to help the needy.[15] In the ab-

13. John Wesley, Sermon 63, "The General Spread of the Gospel," §19, *Sermons II*, ed. Albert C. Outler, *Works*, vol. 2, 493–94.

14. Ibid.

15. A subsistence wage for a male was about one shilling (12 pennies) a day. It is difficult to make an accurate conversion into modern currency, but one can form an idea of how much money this represented by recalling that a full loaf of bread cost about 4 pennies for most of the century and a meal in a London pub might cost 1s. 6d. (18 pennies).

sence of a welfare state, this sort of intervention was often a matter of life and death.

Wesley even set up a small business loan program to help tradesmen and others invest in the means of production so they could become established in a self-supporting way and escape the cycle of poverty. The capital given to these workers could be recycled. Once a worker paid back the loan, the money was available to be loaned to another person in need. James Lackington was one such Methodist in the eighteenth century who had not been able to make a go of it as an apprentice shoemaker. With a loan of five pounds sterling, however, he was able to start a book business in a back lane in London.[16] His was one of the fabulous success stories. By the end of the century, he was selling over one hundred thousand volumes annually, and tourists often stopped to wonder at his shop. It was said that you could drive a coach and six horses around in his showroom.[17]

Unlike Lackington at his most successful, Wesley aspired to the Christian ideal of economic *koinōnia*, as expressed in Acts 2. He believed that if all Christians lived in this way, poverty would come to an end. The third rule for his select societies (small groups for those perfected in love) was that each member should bring all he could spare to a common stock of funds "till we can have all things in common."[18] At least one band of single men sought to live in this way, in an economic commune, seeking to repristinate the ideals of the early church. Wesley himself was determined to give away all he could and to die poor. He did in fact die with £10 to his name once his debts were paid off. Yet he gave away over £30,000 in his lifetime. He once reported that he had two hundred pounds in his pocket,

16. Again, for reference, a careful artisan could hope to keep his family from hunger and out of debt if he earned about one pound a week. A new "two-up and two-down" brick cottage would be worth about £150. See further Roy Porter, *English Social History in the Eighteenth Century* (London: Penguin, 1990), xv.

17. James Lackington, *Memoirs* (London, 1792).

18. John Walsh, "John Wesley and the Community of Goods," in *Protestant Evangelicalism: Britain, Ireland, Germany, and America, c. 1750–c. 1950*, ed. Keith Robbins, Studies in Church History, subsidia, 7 (Oxford: Blackwell, 1990), 41. Cf. Rack, *Reasonable Enthusiast*, 365; and Walsh, *John Wesley*, 16.

"but as life is uncertain," he said, "I will take care to dispose of it before the end of the week."[19]

Wesley regarded the poor as sacred and showed them the highest respect. In a passage in one of his sermons that could have been written by Francis of Assisi or Mother Teresa, he wrote movingly:

> A poor wretch cries to me for an alms: I look and see him covered with dirt and rags. But through these I see one that has an immortal spirit, made to know and love and dwell with God to eternity: I honor him for his Creator's sake. I see through all these rags that he is purpled over with the blood of Christ. I love him for the sake of his Redeemer.[20]

John Walsh wrote that Wesley "tried to re-sacralize the poor in an age in which moralists and economists often saw them only as a problem; as reluctant producers of labour, as a social threat, or at least a nuisance. For Wesley, the indigent were 'poor members of Christ.'"[21]

Salvation of Body and Soul

Wesley reveals a concern not only for the soul but also for the body. The eighteenth century saw some advancement in the treatment of disease, but still it was a period during which far more people died in infancy and youth than in old age. Anaesthetics and antiseptics had not yet been invented, and even

19. Walsh, *John Wesley*, 17; and Rack, *Reasonable Enthusiast*, 361.

20. John Wesley, Sermon 100, "On Pleasing All Men," §2.5, *Works*, vol. 3, 425.

21. Walsh, *John Wesley*, 16. E. P. Thompson's influential and controversial book, *The Making of the English Working Class* (Harmondsworth: Penguin, 1968), portrays Wesley as a Tory paternalist working for the poor rather than with the poor. On this reading, Wesleyan Methodism was a regressive and repressive influence, and its religious discipline molded a preindustrial workforce to accept capitalist time-work discipline without resistance. For a thorough discussion and critique of Thompson's views, see David Hempton and John Walsh, "E. P. Thompson and Methodism," in *God and Mammon: Protestants, Money, and the Market, 1790–1860*, ed. Mark A. Noll (New York: Oxford University Press, 2002), 90–111.

minor ailments could cause acute suffering or lead to a life-threatening condition. There were licensed physicians and surgeons, but the best "physic" that most ill people might hope for was an apothecary, a sort of prescribing pharmacist and common person's general practitioner. Yet even apothecaries were not present in every town and village.

Wesley worried that self-interested physicians and apothecaries were taking advantage of the ill, and he had seen poor people suffer and several families ruined financially without remedy. Since he had long had an interest in anatomy and physic (the art of healing), he determined to do what he could. In 1746, he opened a medical clinic in Bristol and kept office hours on Fridays. "I gave notice of this to the Society," he said, "telling them that all who were ill of chronical distempers . . . might, if they pleased, come to me at such a time, and I would give them the best advice I could and the best medicines I had." He soon followed with free clinics in London and Newcastle as well, creating, it is claimed, the first free dispensaries in England.[22]

Wesley had some success and in due course published his own manual entitled *Primitive Physick; or An Easy and Natural Method of Curing Most Diseases* (1747). The book was exceedingly popular and much reprinted, and many pioneers on the American frontier took it with them as a medical handbook. Wesley combined folk remedies with his own experimental curiosity, and many of the remedies in the manual he vouched for himself and marked "tried." He included some commonsensical treatments, such as applying a cold cloth to a bruise to keep swelling down, and introduced some advanced insights, such as a version of mouth-to-mouth resuscitation for persons who seemed to have drowned. Other remedies were perhaps less straightforward. To cure baldness, for example, he said, "Rub the part morning and evening, with onions, till it is red; and rub it afterward with honey. . . . Or, electrify it daily." To cure a head cold: "Pare very thin the yellow rind of an orange. Roll it up inside out, and thrust a roll into each nostril." Do you have an earache? "Put in a roasted fig, or onion, as hot as may be:

22. This and the following paragraph draw on Richard P. Heitzenrater, *The Elusive Mr. Wesley*, vol. 1, *John Wesley His Own Biographer* (Nashville: Abingdon, 1984), 134–44.

Tried." Or if that doesn't work, "Blow the smoke of tobacco strongly into it." If you have a hernia (I think this is what Wesley meant by a "windy rupture"), "Warm cow-dung well. Spread it thick on leather, strewing some cummin-seeds on it, and apply it hot." You should be as good as new in two days.

Granted, many of these remedies are howlers, but few of us today have as keen a sense as did Wesley of the psychosomatic unity of the needs of those under our spiritual care. It was axiomatic for Wesley that the cure of souls implied the cure of embodied souls, or conversely, ensouled bodies. This was reflected in his treatment of his "patients." He advised them on how to take medicines and to treat themselves according to his manual in a methodical way, but his last point of advice was, "Above all, add to the rest (for it is not labour lost) that old unfashionable medicine, prayer. And have faith in God, who 'killeth and maketh alive, who bringeth down to the grave and bringeth up.'"[23] The popularity of alternative medicine today bears witness to a widespread desire for this sort of integration of mind or spirit and body, though apart from Wesley's sort of orthodox Christianity. Loren Wilkinson discusses in his essay in this volume the "genuine longing for wholeness" in contemporary neo-paganism and the need for Christians to better appreciate that salvation is "a transformation and restoration of our creatureliness." Wesley might have stopped short of defining salvation in this way, but he certainly understood that the Good News of salvation was to be proclaimed by word and deed. And while we may not want to follow his example by rubbing our neighbor's bald pate with onions, we would do well to emulate his concern for the healing of both body and soul.

This care for body and soul can also be seen in the treatment of madness, a condition that caused much debate over spiritual versus natural interpretations. Michel Foucault described the eighteenth century as the period of "the great confinement"; the age of reason, which could not bear unreason, had therefore to remove it from society into asylums.[24] Ac-

23. Ibid., 139.
24. Michel Foucault, *Madness and Civilization: A History of Insanity in the Age of Reason*, trans. R. Howard (New York: Random House, 1973). Cf. Roy Porter, *Mind Forg'd Manacles: A History of Madness in England from the Restoration to the Regency* (London: Penguin, 1987).

cording to this postmodern line of critique, power and knowledge coincided to define the boundaries of sanity and silence
the voice of the unfamiliar other. This was the century during
which Bethlehem hospital, or Bedlam as it was known for
short, gained its reputation as a famous mental asylum in
London. This is not the place to enter into the postmodern debate about reason and unreason in the eighteenth century but
rather to note simply that evangelicals did not reduce the eti-
ology of madness to the simple and stark alternatives of so-
matic and psychosocial causes, on the one hand, or spiritual
causes, on the other.

Certainly, they recognized the possibility of demonization.
Wesley wrote of a gentlewoman whose condition had puzzled
the most eminent physicians for many years, concluding,
"The plain case is, she is tormented by an evil spirit. . . . Yea,
try all your drugs over and over; but at length it will plainly appear that 'this kind goeth not out, but by prayer and fasting.'"[25]
Evangelicals also widely recognized that the travail of conversion involved such a radical reconstitution of identity that
many converts experienced a kind of psychological vertigo
that felt like madness. Jonathan Edwards advised that this
was a place for pastoral sensitivity, especially when dealing
with people with a melancholy constitution, since such souls
under spiritual anxiety could descend into excessive morbid-
ity, causing these people even to take their own lives.[26] A critic
of Methodism, George Lavington, wrote that Methodism had
driven a "number of these unhappy creatures into direct madness and distraction, either of the moaping, or the raving kind."[27]
And Bethlehem hospital actually listed one category of in-
mates (often admitted by family members) as those who were

    25. Wesley, March 10, 1742, *Journals and Diaries II (1738–1743)*, *Works*,
vol. 19, 256.
    26. There was one such notorious suicide in Northampton. See Jonathan
Edwards, *The Works of Jonathan Edwards*, vol. 4, *The Great Awakening*, ed.
C. C. Goen (New Haven: Yale University Press, 1972), 46–47. See further on
Methodism and suicide, Michael Macdonald and Terence R. Murphy, *Sleepless
Souls: Suicide in Early Modern England* (Oxford: Oxford University Press,
1990), 202–3, 324.
    27. George Lavington, *The Enthusiasm of Methodists and Papists Compared*,
vol. 3 (London, 1754), 10.

"Methodistically mad."[28] When John Furz was converted, the local vicar sent his footman with this message: "My master bids me tell you, You have a soft place in your head."[29] Eighteenth-century society did not have much room for anyone who appeared psychologically unstable.

But for Wesley, as for many other evangelicals, conversion involved a deep probing of the human heart. Will there be anything left of me if I let go of myself? Just as an alcoholic has to hit bottom and let go, so also the true convert, taught the evangelicals, had to experience a shattering of the false self. This could lead to powerful displays of agitation. One woman secretly brought a knife with her to a meeting to kill the Methodist preacher Thomas Walsh after his sermon because she had been so overwhelmed with guilt since first hearing him preach. Fortunately for Thomas Walsh, she found peace with God before he finished his message.[30]

Evangelicals thought that madness could also derive simply from constitutional factors. On the whole there seems to have been a wisdom in how Wesley, Whitefield, and other ministers such as John Newton of Olney treated those who were suffering mentally. They did not automatically diabolize madness and proceed to exorcise anyone who appeared deranged. Nor did they just tidy up madness by naturalizing it or by shoving people off into asylums. When John Newton's friend William Cowper descended into psychological crisis in 1773, Newton walked with Cowper; prayed with him and for him; stayed with him, sometimes through the night; allowed him to move into his own house; and helped him seek out medicines and expert medical advice from Dr. Cotton of St. Albans. Newton had one of the early electrical machines that were being used experimentally to treat various ailments, and he even tried this out on Cowper—an early attempt at electroshock therapy. It was all to no avail. Yet Newton did not conclude that Cowper was therefore not in a state of salvation. He wrote on one occasion, "My dear friend still walks in darkness. I can hardly conceive that any one in a state of grace and favour with God can be in greater distress; and

28. Porter, *Mind Forg'd Manacles*, 33.

29. John Telford, ed., *Wesley's Veterans: Lives of Early Methodist Preachers Told by Themselves*, 5 vols. (London: Robert Culley, 1912–14), 5:212.

30. Ibid., 100.

yet no one walked more closely with Him, or was more simply devoted to Him in all things."[31] On another occasion, Newton wrote to
Cowper, saying, "Though your comforts have been so long sus-
pended, I know not that I ever saw you for a single day since your
calamity came upon you, in which I could not perceive . . . that the
grace of God was with you."[32]

This seeming digression into eighteenth-century physic
and mental illness in an essay about evangelical views of salvation reveals the holistic view of the human person among
early evangelicals. God's saving concern extended to those
who suffered in mind, body, or spirit, and therefore, so did the
evangelicals' ministry of the gospel.

The Gospel and Society

Early evangelical concerns were broader than soul saving
not only in terms of the poor and the body but also in terms of
the transformation of society. Their message was narrow, but
their vision was wide. Evangelicalism is often thought of as individualistic, and Wesley's conversion narrative appears to jus-
tify this view. Certainly there was a *pro-me* emphasis, the discovery that the gospel related to me and my concerns uniquely.
But at the same time, we find a surprisingly strong countervailing emphasis on the community of faith—not a lifestyle en-
clave, not a free association of individuals who enter into a con-
tract, not an organization defined by the efficient pursuit of
limited goals but a community that was as much discovered as
it was constructed by human will or agency.

Central to early evangelicalism were the small, intimate
group meetings. With the help of the Pietists, evangelicals almost invented the small group meeting, care group, Bible
study group, Alpha course—whatever you want to call it. They
called them bands, societies, and class meetings. Within these
eighteenth-century cell groups, the fellowship was close, and
men and women could unburden their souls to one another.

31. Josiah Bull, *John Newton of Olney* (London: Religious Tract Society,
1868), 185.
32. John Newton, *Works*, vol. 6 (London, 1808), 162.

Thomas Olivers was one who had heard some Methodist preaching at Bristol, and he was soon in deep spiritual concern for his soul. He began to stalk the Methodists, secretly following them to their meetings and eavesdropping on them. As they sang their hymns, he stood outside crying. When they came out, he followed them at a distance, still listening, sometimes following them for over two miles. He knew they had something he wanted.[33] In Ireland, a mob of ruffians near Wexford wanted to disrupt a Methodist meeting, and so they contrived to hide one of their number inside a sack in the barn where the Methodists met. The plan was for the man to get out of the sack during the meeting, open the barn door, and let the mob in to raise havoc. When the Methodists began singing, however, the man was touched and thought it a pity to disturb them while singing so sweetly. When they prayed, he was moved even more deeply, and he began to cry out under conviction. He got stuck in the sack and lay there bawling and screaming until some from the society let him out. He came out "confessing his sins, and crying for mercy," while his friends pounded on the barn door.[34] Margaret Austin was abused by her husband and then abandoned, left with two children, but eventually she found her way into Methodism after hearing Whitefield. Her desire to join the band meetings was intense, and when she did, she found there the family she had never had. Tellingly, she used kinship language for the woman who nurtured her: "Sister Robinson."[35] When people were converted, they felt they were born again, not in isolation but into a new family of brothers and sisters. It is evident how powerful and attractive was the evangelical sense of *koinōnia*.

John Newton wrote a hymn to dedicate a new meeting place for his religious society, and it includes the stanza:

> Within these walls let holy peace,
> And love, and concord dwell;
> Here give the troubled conscience ease,
> The wounded spirit heal.[36]

33. Telford, *Wesley's Veterans*, 1:210.
34. Ibid., 2:36–37.
35. Margaret Austin to Charles Wesley, ALS, 19 May 1740, Early Methodist Volume, John Rylands Library, Manchester.
36. John Newton and William Cowper, *Olney Hymns* (London, 1779; facsimile reprint, Olney, 1984), 234.

The genre of the hymn itself, a kind of "folksong for Christian folk," was inseparable from the evangelical revival, and the communal nature of the genre points to the importance of such a fellowship.[37] We ought to think of these evangelicals in terms of individuals in the community rather than solely in terms of their private religious experience. Salvation included the whole people of God whom God was calling out and whose spiritual solidarity in Christ was recognized in a new sense of community that could be expressed adequately only in terms of kinship.

Still, was this sense of community sectarian? Was it a "garden walled around," as Isaac Watts famously described Dissenters? The early evangelicals had a vision of the transformation of society and the whole cosmos, as God's kingdom was extended throughout the world, but their vision was one of the gospel spreading, transforming first individuals and then families, Christian nations, and finally non-Christian nations. Thus, Wesley wrote, "In general, it seems, the kingdom of God will not 'come with observation,' but will silently increase wherever it is set up, and spread from heart to heart, from house to house, from town to town, from one kingdom to another."[38] Wesley was clear that this was but a continuation of the evangelical revival he was witnessing:

> All unprejudiced persons may see with their eyes that he is already renewing the face of the earth. And we have strong reason to hope that the work he hath begun he will carry on unto the day of his Lord Jesus; that he will never intermit this blessed work of his Spirit until he has fulfilled all his promises; until he hath put a period to sin and misery, and infirmity, and death; and re-established universal holiness and happiness.[39]

For Wesley, then, the coming of the kingdom was the extension of the reign of God in the hearts of more and more people

37. Erik Routley see hymns and folk songs as different from professional or art songs. Hymns are "communal songs," songs for unmusical people to sing together and poetry for unliterary people to utter together. See further Routley's *Christian Hymns Observed* (Princeton, N.J.: Prestige Publications, 1982), 1–6.

38. Wesley, Sermon 63, "The General Spread of the Gospel," §17, *Works*, vol. 2, 493.

39. Ibid., §27, 499.

until the whole earth was covered with the knowledge of the Lord, as the waters cover the sea. Indeed, this was Wesley's interpretation of the petition "Thy kingdom come" in the Lord's Prayer. "This kingdom then comes," said Wesley, "to a particular person, when he 'repents and believes the gospel.'" The kingdom of God is begun below when it is "set up in the believer's heart" and proceeds to conquer and subdue all things within the human soul. How does this relate to the final and universal sense of the kingdom? Wesley said, "And it is meet for all those who 'love his appearing' to pray that . . . this his kingdom, the kingdom of grace, may come quickly, and swallow up all the kingdoms of the earth."[40] For Wesley, as for Jonathan Edwards in his sermons on the history of redemption, the coming of the kingdom was a matter of the evangelization of larger and larger numbers of individuals. The sense of society being transformed by Christians acting directly on unjust structures in anticipation of the final coming of the kingdom was remote in Wesley's thinking, even while he was involved in numerous practical projects that announced good news for the poor, freedom for the prisoners, sight for the blind, and release for the oppressed.

It is important to recall, however, that most people in *ancien régime* states felt distant from the political process and felt they had little capacity to effect change in the order and structure of society. These were matters of remote providence best left to their betters, they felt, to those charged by God to deal with such questions. Their role was to defer to authority and to pray. To work for a more just society often meant doing what one could in the local milieu. And yet, within their horizon, the early evangelicals not only achieved much but also pioneered new ways of acting in society. Wesley was an early opponent of slavery, and during the late eighteenth century, with the conversion of elites such as William Wilberforce and other members of the so-called Clapham Sect, it became possible for evangelicals to act in an organized way to effect change. Some argue that through their massive organization and mobilization of individuals in auxiliaries across the country and

---

40. John Wesley, Sermon 26, "Upon Our Lord's Sermon on the Mount, Discourse VI," §3.8, *Works*, vol. 1, 582.

their use of petitions in Parliament, evangelicals pioneered modern techniques of eliciting and bringing public opinion to bear on the political process. They understood that political action was the art of the possible and were willing to build co-alitions with others to achieve limited objectives. In this spirit, they were happy to work side by side with the celebrated ora-tor Richard Sheridan, "whether drunk or sober."[41] When, after much struggle, the Abolition of Slavery Bill passed in 1807, Wilberforce went to his friend and neighbor Henry Thornton and said, "Well, Henry, what shall we abolish next?" A new age of political possibilities had dawned for evangelicals.

Salvation and Ecclesiology

The evangelical understanding of the saving work of God implied concern for the poor, the body, and society. Wesley understood that the gospel demanded such comprehensive in-terests. It is thus possible to appreciate that a narrow evange-listic message might yet have wide implications. Moreover, notwithstanding the inflexibility and decisiveness of his evan-gelistic preaching, Wesley held to a theology of salvation that had a breadth and charity that included the salvation of mem-bers of other communions. This was true for other early evan-gelicals as well. Indeed, both Wesley and Whitefield wrote about what they called a "catholic spirit" and extolled the fel-lowship of all those who had experienced new birth. In 1741 in Scotland, the Associate Presbytery of the Erskine brothers asked Whitefield to preach only for them, as they were truly the Lord's people. Whitefield repudiated this separatism in favor of transdenominationalism, saying, "If the Pope himself would lend me his pulpit, I would gladly proclaim the righ-teousness of Jesus Christ therein."[42] John Newton wrote to a more broad-minded member of a secessionist church in Scot-land some years later and said, "My heart is . . . more espe-cially with those who, like you, can look over the pales of an

41. Ernest Marshall Howse, *Saints in Politics* (London: Allen and Unwin, 1971), 135.
42. George Whitefield, *Works*, vol. 1, ed. John Gillies (London, 1771), 308.

enclosure, and rejoice in the Lord's work where he is pleased to carry it on under some difference of forms."[43] Wesley aspired after similar ideals. "My only question at present is this," he said. "Is thine heart right, as my heart is with thy heart?"[44] Wesley did not dissolve doctrine into experience, since he followed his appeal with an exposition of what it meant to have a heart right with God, which involved fundamental doctrine.[45] Still, because of this focus on lived faith, Whitefield, Newton, and Wesley recognized true believers among Dissenters, Catholics, and Orthodox. Newton wrote, for example, "If such persons as Fenelon, Pascal, Quesnell, and Nicole (to mention no more), were not true Christians, where shall we find any who deserve the name?" Such as these "might do honour to the most enlightened Protestant."[46] Effectively, he was willing to grant them honorary evangelical membership.

This sort of thinking represented a significant development in the modern world, an ecclesiology that transcended the national churches. The ecclesiology of the confessional state or territorial church derived from the magisterial Reformation. It allowed one to color England pink on the map because it was Anglican, or to color Scotland purple because it was Calvinist, or Spain yellow because it was Catholic. In contrast, the evangelicals participated in that new form of pietism that acknowledged a union of all those from various Christian traditions who were truly regenerated in Christ.[47] Therefore, if I believe in election and you do not, I can still believe you are elect. If I believe in justification by faith and you do not, I can still believe you have the faith that justifies. By various formulae such as these, evangelical leaders tried to affirm a new kind of ecumenism without dissolving the distinctions of the visible churches. Salvation was larger than adherence to a rightly ordered visible church.

43. John Newton, *Original Letters from the Reverend John Newton . . . to the Rev. W. Barlass* (New York, 1819), 49.

44. John Wesley, Sermon 39, "Catholic Spirit," §11, *Works*, vol. 2, 87.

45. Ibid., §§12–13.

46. Newton, *Works*, vol. 5, 29. (I have modernized the spelling of the names in this quotation: Newton's original was "De Fenelon, Paschall, Quenell, and Nicole.")

47. See further F. Ernest Stoeffler, *The Rise of Evangelical Pietism*, Studies in the History of Religions, 9 (Leiden: E. J. Brill, 1965).

Salvation: Initiation and Completion

The final area in which early evangelical concerns extended beyond simple soul saving was in their theology of conversion. Wesley was resolute that salvation was not from the punishment of sin but from sin. His doctrine of entire sanctification or perfection was controversial then, as now, but it leant to his whole order of salvation a strongly teleological sense of salvation. The hymn "Love Divine, All Loves Excelling," which has been sung so politely at so many weddings by the well-meaning sister of the bride, was included in the Wesley brothers' hymnbook under the heading "Seeking for Full Redemption," and it expresses the fervent longing of many Methodists to know here and now the fullness of salvation. When listening to the lyrics of this hymn, we must think of the perfectionist revivals of the mid-eighteenth century at which women and men cried out that they had been sanctified, and others longed for the same experience in tears and groaning. The lines "Fix in us thy humble dwelling" and "Visit us with thy salvation" are cries of invocation, not words of decorative poetry. Recall the last stanza:

> Finish then thy new creation,
>   Pure and spotless let us be;
> Let us see thy great salvation,
>   Perfectly restored in thee;
> Changed from glory into glory,
>   Till in heaven we take our place,
> Till we cast our crowns before thee,
>   Lost in wonder, love, and praise.[48]

The goal of salvation was nothing less than "that holiness without which no one will see the Lord." Increasingly, Wesley emphasized faith as a means to the end of holiness: *Fides caritatem formata*, "faith working by love," became the center of his theology of salvation.[49] Perfection, though, was a contested point even among his own followers. William Grimshaw of

48. Charles Wesley, "Love Divine, All Loves Excelling," in *A Collection of Hymns for the Use of the People Called Methodists*, ed. Franz Hildebrandt, Oliver A. Beckerlegge, and James Dale, *Works*, vol. 7, 547.

49. Stephen Gunter, *The Limits of "Love Divine": John Wesley's Response to Antinomianism and Enthusiasm* (Nashville: Abingdon, 1989), 270–76.

Haworth would have none of it. When some claimed to be perfected, he said, "I wish they knew their own hearts. My perfection is to see my own imperfection. . . . I know no other, expecting to lay down my Life and my Sword together."[50] And yet other evangelicals picked up this teleological drive in Wesley's understanding of salvation. Newton wrote to a friend in 1772 saying that he was far, very far, from maintaining this idea of sinless perfection, "yet there is a liberty and privilege attainable by the Gospel, beyond what is normally thought of. Per words, there are undreamt of possibilities in the spiritual life in terms of how God might indeed transform believers before death into holy persons. To another correspondent he laid out a series of typical stages in Christian experience from the initiation of faith to an experience of contemplative union with Christ, which is about as close as he could be to Wesley's thinking without ceasing to be a Calvinist.[51]

This sense of "a liberty and privilege attainable by the Gospel" is the larger sense of salvation I would like to stress, since it contrasts with predominant images of evangelicalism today that focus on one-time decisions made in the context, for example, of crusade evangelism. Evangelicals in the past have often understood salvation to include what Catholics call ascetical theology, or what many today would describe as formative spirituality. Salvation has a past, a present, and a future tense.

Conclusion: Evangelical Soteriology and the Human Heart

To sum up, the life and ministry of John Wesley, and those of a few other early evangelicals, reveal that the evangelical sense of what it meant to proclaim and live the gospel, to announce God's salvation to the world, embraced a broader perspective than we might have expected given the characterization today that evangelicals are concerned only with saving souls.

50. Frank Baker, *William Grimshaw* (London: Epworth, 1963), 74.
51. Ibid., 171–91.

Yet after all of this has been said, I do in fact want to concede that Wesley and other evangelicals conceived of salvation primarily (and that is an important adverb) in terms of the individual and his or her eternal destiny. They understood that the gospel implied much else, but when they spoke of salvation, they conceived of it primarily in terms of the inherited Reformed ordo—the so-called golden chain of God's saving actions that begin and end in eternity: Those whom God predestines, he calls, justifies, sanctifies, and glorifies. Even Wesley is best understood, I think, as working within this Reformed order of salvation with his own reinterpretation of the terms. This ordo defines God's saving acts, and there are corresponding human responses such as faith and repentance. Herein lay the main lines of debate in the eighteenth century. The chief debates among evangelicals came down time and again to the relationship between divine and human agency in the order of salvation. What is God's role, and what is the human role? Wesley was seen by most eighteenth-century evangelicals to have pushed as far as was acceptable toward the human pole. It was assumed by all, however, that to collapse the dialectic between divine and human agency entirely around one pole or the other was to place one outside an evangelical theology of salvation. To aver outright self-salvation was legalism; to contend for divine coercion to the abolishment of the human will was antinomianism.[52] I wonder if these two boundary markers do not still define the borders within which evangelicals are willing to embrace acceptable soteriological proposals and to ask questions when evaluating proposals. In any case, it has been the main problematic debated within the evangelical theology of salvation for many generations.

The sense of early evangelicals such as Wesley, Whitefield, and Edwards that the salvation construed in these terms had to do primarily with individuals must, however, be seen in context. It must be seen in the context of an *ancien régime* society with an Established Church that still had the overwhelm-

---

52. See further my discussion of eighteenth-century evangelical theology in Bruce Hindmarsh, *John Newton and the English Evangelical Tradition* (Oxford: Clarendon, 1996), 120–25.

ing support of the population, a context in which most people were baptized and regarded themselves as Christian in the way that I regard myself as Canadian: I emerged into a consciousness of my citizenship without ever thinking about it as a conscious choice. Christendom still cast its shadow over eighteenth-century society in such a way that most men and women regarded it as their duty (whether they fulfilled this duty or not) to "go to church and sacrament" and to "do no harm." Evangelicalism represented a protest against the idea that adhering to Christian civil society as a nominal Christian was sufficient for salvation.[53] Evangelicalism emerged precisely on the trailing edge of Christendom and the leading edge of modernity. Enough scope had opened for individual agency that an appeal could be made to men and women to respond knowingly and personally to the gospel message. No wonder so many regarded it as a message not heard before. But their protest is not ours. Whereas we now protest against an excessive individualism in the old age of modernism, they were protesting against an excessively corporate but nominal view of salvation in the old age of Christendom. We worry that our typical understanding of salvation is deeply individual but not broad; they worried that the typical understanding of salvation was broad but not deeply individual.

Viewed in terms of this sort of cultural history, the story takes on a necessary hourglass shape. The early evangelicals narrowed salvation from Christian civil society and its corporate rituals to the individual and the human heart, but this was a necessary narrowing and deepening to repristinate the gospel in personal terms. This was necessary so that the gospel could be heard afresh. The evangelicals were, after all, concerned about the evangel, not about advancing a partisan organization. From this point forward the gospel could advance, as Wesley hoped, from heart to heart, house to house, and town to town. We stand in the process of time, and this

53. Cf. Andrew Walls, "The Evangelical Revival, The Missionary Movement, and Africa," in *Evangelicalism*, ed. Mark Noll, David Bebbington, and George Rawlyk (New York: Oxford University Press, 1994), 310–30. Walls writes, for example, "The evangelicalism of the period takes its identity from protest, and in effect from nominal Christianity. Evangelical religion presupposes Christendom, Christian civil society" (312).

hourglass movement has preceded our discussion, freeing us
to think about the character of God's great salvation in ways
that Wesley might not have imagined but with a shared sense
of personal response to the gospel.

We return, then, to Wesley's "strangely warmed heart," the
evangelical topos with which we began. But we can now see,
in the light of Wesley's own concerns and the necessary protest in which he was engaged, that the heart was not a symbol
of narrowness or private piety. It was, as the Book of Proverbs
says, the wellspring of life. Pseudo-Macarius, a fourth-century
ascetic, loved by Wesley, put it this way: "The heart itself is but
a small vessel, yet dragons are there, and there are also lions;
there are poisonous beasts and all the treasures of evil. . . . But
there too is God, the angels, the life and the Kingdom, the light
and the apostles, the heavenly cities and the treasuries of
grace—all things are there."[54] The human heart, it turns out, is
broad and spacious. The early evangelicals were concerned
that salvation, whatever else it was, had to do with the heart.
These are ancient paths we dare not leave.

---

54. George A. Maloney, trans. and ed., *Pseudo-Macarius*, Classics of Western Spirituality (New York: Paulist Press, 1992), xvi.

3

Agnus Victor

The Atonement as Victory and Vicarious Punishment

Henri A. G. Blocher

"A mighty fortress is our God, a bulwark never failing. . . . Did we in our own strength confide, our striving would be losing. . . . Were not the right man on our side, the man of God's own choosing. . . ." The proclamation of Jesus Christ's victory over the powers of evil vibrates in Christian hymns, and preachers have often cast the Good News of salvation in the language of a supra-cosmic duel between God in Christ and the devil, resulting in the latter's defeat and the consequent liberation of those he had kept in bondage.

The Lutheran theologian from Lund, Gustaf Aulén (1879–1977), gained worldwide fame when he claimed in 1930 that this was the "classic" view of the atonement—he also called it the "dramatic" view—and complained in his book *Christus Victor* that it had been disregarded in the Western tradition and

unfortunately replaced by the "Latin" view, a juridical con-
struct with "satisfaction" as a key concept.[1] Only Martin Luther
had been able to recover the authentic "victory" notion, but
Protestant orthodoxy after him had relapsed into the "Latin"
view.[2]

The emphasis in recent years on spiritual warfare would appear to add fresh relevance to the interpretation of the atonement in terms of struggle, conquest, and triumph.[3] Cultures
characterized by an acute awareness of the spirit world and the
oppressive activity of its invisible agents may also value the "polemic" scheme (as I prefer to call it, from polemos, fight, strife,
warfare). The young theologian from Mali, Youssouf Dembélé,
has recently made a strong biblical case for restoring this interpretation to primacy.[4]

If one lays stress on the atonement (Christ's work of salvation) as conquest and triumph over the enemy, one meets,
rather sooner than later in the evangelical regions of Christendom, the traditional focus on penal substitution as the main
meaning of the cross. Preaching salvation as wrought, full and
complete, by the punishment Christ underwent vicariously on
our behalf, has been the hallmark of evangelicalism for several
centuries, and John Stott has been able to defend it eloquently

1. Aulén first delivered lectures on his topic at Uppsala University and published Den kristna försoningstanken in Swedish and the article "Die drei Haupt-
typen des christlichen Versöhnungsgedankens," in Zeitschrist für Systematische
Theologie 8 (1930): 501–38. His book was translated into English by A. G. Her-
bert, Christus Victor: An Historical Study of the Three Main Types of the Idea of
the Atonement (1931; reprint, London: S.P.C.K., 1961). See also the French version: Christus Victor. La notion chrétienne de rédemption, trans. G. Hoffmann-
Sigel (Paris: Aubier, 1949).

2. Ibid., 139–44 (in the French version, which appears to be quite different
in this part of the book; also 26–29).

3. See C. Peter Wagner, Warfare Prayer: How to Seek God's Power and Pro-
tection in the Battle to Build His Kingdom (Ventura, Calif.: Regal, 1992); and
C. Peter Wagner and F. Douglas Pennoyer, eds., Wrestling with Dark Angels:
Toward a Deeper Understanding of the Supernatural Forces in Spiritual Warfare
(Ventura, Calif.: Regal, 1990); also Gregory A. Boyd, God at War: The Bible and
Spiritual Conflict (Downers Grove, Ill.: InterVarsity, 1997).

4. "Salvation as Victory: A Reconsideration of the Concept of Salvation in
the Light of Jesus Christ's Life and Work Viewed as a Triumph over the Personal Powers of Evil" (Ph.D. diss., Trinity Evangelical Divinity School, Deer-
field, Illinois, 2001).

against current criticisms.[5] How should we regard the relationship between the two schemes or accounts? Are they *mutually
exclusive?* Aulén thinks this is the case, as his aversion to the
"Latin" doctrine quite clearly implies.[6] Are they to be *maintained jointly,* without one being derived from the other and
both on the same footing? This seems to be Dembélé's choice,
though he tends to put the "act of power" first.[7] Are we to *subordinate* the polemic scheme (since we will not discard it) to
penal substitution? This is what J. I. Packer proposes: "Christ's
death had its effect first on God, who was hereby *propitiated*
(or, better, who hereby propitiated himself), and only because
it had this effect did it become an overthrowing of the powers
of darkness."[8] This chapter aims at finding an answer to this set
of questions, remembering the great rule laid down by Packer:
"All our understanding of the cross comes from attending to the
biblical witnesses and learning to hear and echo what they say
about it; speculative rationalism [and I would add, under diverse guises] breeds only misunderstanding, nothing more."[9]

The Polemic Scheme and Its Doctrinal Weight

Aulén's work was a landmark in historical theology, and therefore, it remains the obvious reference, though not the only reference, when evaluating the *Christus Victor* representation of the
atonement as a theological account of scriptural teaching.

5. *The Cross of Christ* (Leicester: Inter-Varsity, 1987).
6. In *Christus Victor,* 31, he calls it "only a side-track," which implies he
would not grant it a rightful place.
7. "Salvation as Victory," 332, rules out subordination. "Jesus' victory over
Satan is not subordinated to his victory over sin but rather the two victories
are two operations of the same war" (340). He charges Packer with reversing
the true order (284f., 332f.; similarly William G. T. Shedd, 280). Dembélé further argues that "the person [Satan] has primacy over his works [sin]" (261,
quoting Heb. 3:3 in support) and draws from the parable of the strong man
bound, a major text in his argument, that Jesus *first* gains his mastery over Satan through an act of power and *then* is able to do the work of redemption
(262).
8. "What Did the Cross Achieve? The Logic of Penal Substitution," *Tyndale Bulletin* 25 (1974): 20: What "grounds man's plight as a victim" is divine judgment.
9. Ibid., 36.

Conflict and Victory, Yes

One can hardly deny the weighty presence of polemic language and pictures in the biblical witness to the divine work of atonement[10] and the comparative deficit, in this regard, in the teaching of the churches, including evangelical churches. (The deficit would probably be less in a comparison with evangelical *preaching:* Whereas handbooks of doctrine and even catechisms do not devote much space to Christ's victory over the foe, it has been loudly proclaimed from the pulpit. Statistical evidence cannot be offered, but remembrances from the preaching of Charles H. Spurgeon or Billy Graham or even John Calvin lend some authority to that estimate. The reason for the difference might be this: The polemic theme suits well the preacher's stance, for it provides *obvious* Good News and focuses on the effects and existential benefits of the atonement; it is less helpful when one seeks understanding, when one inquires about the *how* of the atonement and its necessity—as the following analysis will show.)

The *Christus Victor* plea reminds us that "to this end the Son of God appeared: in order to dissolve the works of the devil" (1 John 3:8, author's translation); that he came to share in flesh and blood so as to be able to rescue and free those who were, all their lives and by means of the fear of death, enslaved by the devil (Heb. 2:14–15); that the cross was the place where he disarmed the (spiritual and evil) powers and authorities and triumphed over them (Col. 2:15); that our Lord himself explained that he could free men and women from the grip of demons by virtue of his victory over Satan (Mark 3:27 and parallels); and that the event for which he came into the world would mean the "casting out" of the prince of this world (John 12:31) and the latter's condemnation (John 16:11). It also illuminates the Easter side of the saving event, the overcoming of death forever.

Polemic language is typical of apocalyptic literature, and Jesus Christ's Revelation to John is no exception: It talks much of the war

10. Dembélé's strength in "Salvation as Victory" lies in his rich demonstration of that presence, whereas Aulén deals only in cursory fashion with New Testament evidence (he speaks of a "brief glance" himself, *aperçu rapide,* in the French version of *Christus Victor,* 115).

that the Beast with its horns is waging against the Lamb, and "the Lamb will defeat them, for he is Lord of lords and King of kings" (Rev. 17:14 NEB). The *Christus Victor* perspective suits the famous dictum that "apocalyptic is the mother of all Christian theology"! C. H. Dodd's proposal undoubtedly deserves a hearing: The Lamb, even in the Fourth Gospel (John 1:29, 36), is the warrior-lamb of Jewish apocalypses, the young and vigorous ram with horns, "the prince and leader of the sheep" (*1 Enoch* 89:46, the *Testament of the Twelve, Joseph* 19:8 being the other key passage he quotes), Messiah victorious.[11] Indeed, the seven-horned Lamb of Revelation 5 is none other than the victorious Lion of Judah (Rev. 5:5). In Dodd's estimate, even the clause "who takes away *[airōn]* the sin of the world" (John 1:29) may be interpreted as the mere removal of all sins, which Messiah will accomplish by force, and "it would seem to be by no means impossible that it may have been used, in its apocalyptic sense, by John the Baptist."[12] Beyond the background of the apocalyptic trend in Judaism, the *Christus Victor* theme also provides continuity with a main Old Testament theme: that of YHWH as the champion of righteousness who overpowers all his enemies.[13] "Who is this King of glory? YHWH strong and valiant, YHWH valiant at war!" (Ps. 24:8, author's translation).

The polemic scheme normally involves the recognition that superhuman agents of evil are real. The defeated foes, bearing the names Satan and his angels (evil spirits or demons, principalities and powers), should not be considered mere symbols of human passions (individual or social) or oppressive structures. Nor, ultimately, should they be considered a "tragic" dimension in the metaphysical fabric of the universe. It would exceed the scope of this study even to begin arguing in favor of this traditional tenet, but I wish to declare, against demythologized interpretations, that Satan and demons are names for quasi-personal beings endowed

11. *The Interpretation of the Fourth Gospel* (1953; reprint, Cambridge: University of Cambridge Press, 1968), 231f., 236–38.
12. Ibid., 238. On page 237 he offers the following references on the forcible removal of sin: *Test. of Levi* 18:9; *Ps. of Solomon* 17:29; *Apoc. of Baruch* 73:1–4.
13. The third chapter in Dembélé, "Salvation as Victory," is devoted to "Yahweh, a God of war and salvation." He can marshall much evidence from the Old Testament; unfortunately, he does not raise the hermeneutical question of the New Covenant correspondence or antitype of the wars of YHWH.

with distinctive existence[14] and, further, against Karl Barth, that they were created by God (Rom. 8:38f.; Col. 1:16) and therefore must have "fallen" at one point, forsaking their own "principle" *(archē)* and place (Jude 6).[15] The term *"quasi* personal" means that their personhood, an analogical notion, is realized far differently than in human persons (and in the Persons of the divine

14. Paul's meaning is soberly defined by Daniel G. Reid: "The understanding of powers existing as angelic servants of God is well represented in texts reflecting the Judaism of Paul's day, and the notion that some of these are 'fallen,' hostile spiritual beings is also found. It seems likely that Paul understood the powers to belong to the latter category, and that he did attribute to them a spiritual, ontological existence" ("Principalities and Powers," in *Dictionary of Paul and His Letters*, ed. Gerald F. Hawthorne and Ralph P. Martin [Downers Grove, Ill.: InterVarsity; Leicester: Inter-Varsity, 1993], 750). See also Clinton E. Arnold, *Ephesians: Power and Magic. The Concept of Power in Ephesians in Light of Its Historical Setting* (Grand Rapids: Baker, 1992), with the decisive reply to Walter Wink, 48ff., 132; idem, "Satan, Devil," in *Dictionary of the Later New Testament and Its Developments*, ed. Ralph P. Martin and Peter H. Davids (Downers Grove, Ill.: InterVarsity; Leicester: Inter-Varsity, 1997), 1077–82; and Peter T. O'Brien, "Principalities and Powers: Opponents of the Church," in *Biblical Interpretation and the Church: Text and Context*, ed. Donald A. Carson (Exeter: Paternoster, 1984), 110–50. I beg to differ on the *stoicheia* (elements); in my opinion, the more common view underestimates the fact that *no occurrence* of the word for star spirits (nor for local deities) has yet been found before the second and third century, and Eduard Schweizer's arguments are much more impressive in his "Die 'Elemente der Welt' Gal 4,3.9; Kol 2,8.20," *Beiträge zur Theologie des Neuen Testaments* (Zurich and Stuttgart: Zwingli Verlag, 1970), 147–63. I also deny that there is solid ground for identifying "the princes of this age" in 1 Corinthians 2:6–9 as heavenly powers (agreeing with Victor P. Hamilton, "Satan," in *Anchor Bible Dictionary*, vol. 5, ed. David Noel Freedman [New York: Doubleday, 1992], 988, who refers to Wesley Carr, "Rulers of this Age," *New Testament Studies* 23 [1976]: 20–35). *Nowhere* in the New Testament is the plural *archontes* (princes, rulers) used for heavenly principalities; nowhere are these latter said to have crucified the Lord; nowhere, even, is a "wisdom" ascribed to them in express terms.

15. Barth's interpretation of the devil and demons as "real" but having no being, as figures of *das Nichtige* (nothingness, non-being), involves such a different frame of reference (theological paradigm) that I cannot discuss his views here. Paul Tillich stands even farther away from realism, yet he does retain a polemic element: Being-itself eternally overcomes Non-Being within itself, and we are to understand the New Being as the existential appropriation of this "victory" (the fount of the courage to be); the medium, for us Christians, is Jesus as the Christ (not necessarily the historical Jesus), who negated himself as *a* being for the sake of Being-itself. I cannot deal with such speculations in this study.

Trinity). I remain agnostic on several particulars of this issue, but the main proposition is clear, and proclaiming the atonement as victory advantageously promotes biblical realism as to the world of spirits.[16]

Analytical Inadequacies

Despite the assets just considered, Aulén's version of the polemic scheme is vulnerable in the very development of its analysis. Central is the antithesis of "interrupted" (broken) and "uninterrupted" (unbroken) operations: Aulén claims that, for the "dramatic" view, the divine salvific action is uninterrupted, while the legal order is interrupted or broken; for the "Latin" view, the divine action is interrupted, and the legal order is granted permanent validity.[17] Are these gross or rough categories helpful? The symmetry is misleading. Whether in Anselm's or in B. B. Warfield's doctrine, the statement that the divine salvific action is interrupted or broken cannot be sustained. The idea that the legal order is broken (even exploded) when atonement takes place may suit Aulén's rather antinomian bent, but it would be difficult to find in any of the major witnesses of patristic thought and Reformation doctrine. Paul Althaus, one of the sharpest minds of German Lutheranism, soon perceived that Aulén's categorical pair was inadequate and replied that Luther did *not* teach that the order of divine law had

16. Human personhood is essentially bound to community, rooted in the organic unity of humankind and belonging together, and this may be a reflection of the trinitarian One. Nothing of the kind exists (it seems) for angels, who are not bound to one another genealogically, through sharing a common nature; angels are pure individuals, each one of them having a distinctive nature. Human personhood, also, is expressed in the bodily condition, in which invisible spirits have no share. Is it required for community? It is a fact that the organic unity of the human race comes about through bodily reproduction and functions through the use of bodily signs, above all those of language; human beings jointly possess, or belong to, the same "third term," earthly matter; it may be the only way for created spirits, who, as such, are external to one another, to achieve a high degree of organic togetherness. This is not necessary for God's personal life: The Persons of the Trinity are not external to one another but absolutely One in mutual indwelling, *perichōrēsis*. (Differences between human persons and angels may entail both superiorities and inferiorities.)

17. Aulén, *Christus Victor,* 21f., 105, 147.

been broken.[18] Aulén's arrangement of the data inevitably distorts them.

A related misunderstanding (not Aulén's only) affects the status of the law in Pauline theology. Aulén claims that the apostle puts the law among the harmful powers, which must be broken.[19] This is a road that leads to Marcionite perdition! Aulén is compelled to acknowledge the primacy of juridical concerns in the Old Testament, and he then comments: "It is, however, exactly at this point that the emergence of the classic idea of redemption [i.e., his] in the New Testament shows how radical the breach between Judaism and Christianity is."[20] In all fairness, it must be observed that these unfortunate associations of Aulén's choice are not to be imputed to all advocates of the *Christus Victor* emphasis.

Historical Coloring

Inadequate conceptual tools and presuppositions breed historical misrepresentation. Calling the view he champions "classical" may be seen as a clever tactical move on the part of Aulén, but such a label lacks proper warrant from the texts! Impressions gained through ordinary acquaintance with the writings of the fathers converge with stated conclusions of authorities in the field: (1) The polemic presentation of the work of salvation is popular indeed (mostly in "popular" preaching!), but it is only one among several; (2) even when the theme is the victory won over the devil, the fathers, starting with Irenaeus and his *Adversus haereses* V.1.1.,[21] are

18. *Die Theologie Martin Luthers*, 6th ed. (Gütersloh: Gerd Mohn, 1983), 193f., according to Tobias Eißler (who agrees with Althaus), "Die Heilstat Jesu Christi in altkirchlicher, mittelalterlicher und reformatorischer Sicht," in *Warum das Kreuz? Die Frage nach der Bedeutung des Todes Jesu*, ed. Volker Gäckle (Tübingen and Wuppertal: R. Brockhaus, 1998), 127 n. 40. I regret B. Sesboüé's leniency or sympathy for Aulén's categories in his *Histoire des dogmes, tome I: le Dieu du salut*, ed. Bernard Sesboüé and Joseph Wolinski (Paris: Desclée, 1994), 453f.

19. Aulén, *Christus Victor*, 83–85.

20. Ibid., 95.

21. Ibid., 43f. Aulén notices Irenaeus's concern but does not draw the consequences; he interprets the way God chose to avoid infringing on the rights of justice (in Irenaeus's passage), the way of "persuasion" *(secundum suadelam)*, as implying that Christ surrendered himself to the devil as the ransom of humankind. I suggest the more probable object of the persuasion is human (because of the emphasis on obedience as the weapon elsewhere, esp. V.21 and

acutely concerned to show that God upheld and did not break the standards of justice; and (3) the language of judicial substitution, of the legal debt that was paid by the precious blood of the Son of God, is by no means rare among the fathers (though it does not possess the Reformation centrality and clarity). Jean Rivière could write that "penal substitution" and "expiatory sacrifice" "represent the two fundamental directions of the Fathers' theology of atonement";[22] Eusebius of Caesarea was able to bring the two into unity, as he saw penal substitution as the heart of sacrifice.[23] Adolf von Harnack wrote, "While the Incarnation was always presupposed, in the West, the death of Christ became the *punctum saliens*. Already before St. Augustine it is considered, more or less, under all possible aspects: as a sacrifice, as reconciliation, as a ransom, as penal substitution. St. Ambrose uncovers its relationship to sin conceived of as a debt."[24] Rivière protests that the same is true of the Greek fathers.[25] Apart from the famous passage of the *Epistle to Diognetus* IX:2–4 that extolls the "sweet exchange,"[26] Origen stressed the need

---

III.18.7). The immediate context speaks of redemption by Christ's blood, as he "gave his soul for our souls, his flesh for our flesh" (V.1.1, cf. 2.1). Aulén rightly sees that the same concern for justice on God's part produced the various theories on the rights of the demon and how he forfeited them. Several fathers imagined that Satan had gained, through human disobedience, some kind of property rights over the world (sometimes using Luke 4:6 as a proof-text) and that God had to respect them, but Satan lost them as he committed the major injustice of crucifying the righteous one. Augustine himself offered a refined version of such theories in his *De Trinitate* XIII.xiv.18, xv.19.

22. *Le Dogme de la rédemption. Etude théologique*, 3rd ed. (Paris: Lecoffre-Gabalda, 1931), 96.

23. Ibid., 97, referring to the *Demonstratio evangelica* X.1 (Migne's *Patrologia graeca* 22:724f.).

24. *Dogmengeschichte II:* 50f., as quoted (and translated into French) by Rivière, ibid., 82.

25. Rivière, *Dogme de la rédemption*, 82ff., 93f. Similarly, Eißler, "Die Heilstat Jesu Christi," 115.

26. I am using Henri-Irénée Marrou, *A Diognète. Introduction, édition critique, traduction et commentaire*, rev. ed. (coll. Sources chrétiennes n° 33bis; Paris: Cerf, 1965); the passage is found on 74 and Marrou's translation on 75. I offer the following translation, based on Marrou's French one and the original: "[IX:2] He did not hate us neither did he reject us, nor did he bear resentment against us. On the contrary, he showed himself forbearing and patient and mercifully took upon himself our sins. Himself, he gave his own son as a ransom *[lytron]* for us, the holy one for the transgressors, the innocent one for the evil, the righ-

for a propitiatory sin offering that was offered for the whole world;[27] Athanasius first systematized and was able to develop the *logic* of penal substitution with the argument that God must be true to his word and that Christ's death paid the debt—*ekplērou to opheilomenon en tō thanatō* ("in, or by, death, he paid to the full what was due").[28] Chrysostom leaves nothing to ambiguity: "Men ought to be punished; God did not punish them; they were to perish: God gave his Son in their stead *(ant' ekeinōn)."*[29] Of course, one could also find many expressions of the so-called physical theory of salvation. There were several "classical" views!

Further, one could dispute Aulén's reading of medieval theology, but the main correction that is called for concerns Luther's theology. Tobias Eißler shows that Luther used the concepts of right, satisfaction, legal payment, and merit as the scholastics had done.[30] He quotes Luther's own words: "Christ had to be a priest and, according to the sacerdotal office, reconcile us to God: it was necessary that he should satisfy God's justice; because there was no other satisfaction, he had to offer himself, to die, and thus to overcome sin together with death in himself."[31] And again in a sermon: "For our sakes . . . ; he became a curse for us, he bore God's

---

teous one for the unrighteous, the incorruptible one for the corruptible, the immortal one for the mortal. [3] For, what else but the righteousness of that One was able to cover *[kalypsai]* our sins? [4] Who else but the only Son of God could make it possible that we, the lawless and godless, be justified? [5] O the sweet exchange *[antallagē]*! O the unsearchable achievement! O the unexpected benefits! The iniquity of many is thus hidden in one righteous, and the righteousness of one justifies many transgressors." Marrou's commentary on the word *antallagē* is worth quoting: "Rather than to a merely subjective effect of justification, this word appears to refer to an objective transformation of the human situation in relationship to God" (200), and in note 1, he stresses that *hyper,* in the passage, bears the substitutive sense.

27. Ibid., 96, quoting *In Num.* hom. 24 (*Patr. gr.* 12:757f.).

28. *De Incarnatione Verbi,* 4–10 (the phrase quoted is from section 9, in J. Tixeront, *Histoire des dogmes de l'antiquité chrétienne II: de saint Athanase à saint Augustin,* 9th ed. [Paris: Lecoffre-Gabalda, 1931], 152).

29. *In epist. I ad Timotheum,* hom. VII,3, as quoted in Tixeront, *Histoire des dogmes,* 152.

30. Eißler, "Die Heilstat Jesu Christi," 127.

31. Weimar Ausgabe 10 I/1, 720:18ff., as cited (in a German version) in ibid., 128.

wrath, he wanted to pay for our sin, that we may reach the bless-ing, receive the Holy Spirit, that we may be clear of sins and be-come children of God."[32] Luther, of course, endorsed the Augs-burg Confession, whose article IV in the Latin text uses *satisfactio*.

Biblical Subtraction

Aulén's aversion to what he calls the "Latin" view prevented him from identifying the place that schemes other than *Christus Victor* occupy in Scripture. It is a weakness that he leaves out large segments of the canonical witness. The key confession throughout the New Testament is, "Christ died for our sins ac-cording to the Scriptures" (1 Cor. 15:3), and the devil is not even mentioned in "strategic" passages such as Romans 3:21–26, 2 Corinthians 5:11–21, and Hebrews 1:1–3, 9–10. In the more didactic parts, the predominance of juridical and liturgi-cal languages may generally be observed. Elsewhere I have countered efforts at minimizing or erasing penal substitution in the Bible.[33] Suffice it for now to quote a well-inspired com-ment on the Fourth Isaianic Servant Song, Isaiah 52:13–53:12:

> [This passage] makes twelve distinct and explicit statements that the Servant suffers the *penalty* of other men's sins: not only vicarious suffering but penal substitution is the plain meaning of its fourth, fifth and sixth verses. These may not be precise statements of Western forensic ideas but they are clearly related with penalty, inflicted through various forms of punishment which the Servant endured on other men's behalf and in their stead, because the Lord so ordained. This legal or law-court metaphor of atonement may be stated positively or negatively: either as penalty which the Redeemer takes upon himself, or as acquittal which sets the prisoner free. But in either way of stat-ing it the connotation is substitutionary: "In my place con-demned he stood; / Sealed my pardon with his blood."[34]

32. Sermon on Matt. 27:33–56, Weimar Ausgabe 52, 807:10ff., as quoted in ibid., 129.
33. "The Sacrifice of Jesus Christ: The Current Theological Situation," *European Journal of Theology* 8, no. 1 (1999): 23–36.
34. J. S. Whale, *Victor and Victim* (Cambridge: University of Cambridge Press, 1960), 69f., as quoted in Packer, "What Did the Cross Achieve?" 34 n. 36.

Logical Questions

The foregoing considerations preclude making the polemic scheme the "classical" one and render it unlikely that it could function as the main paradigm for doctrine. The fact that questions arise as soon as one starts searching for understanding (fides quaerens intellectum) confirms that tentative conclusion.

The main query is basic indeed: How is the battle fought and the victory gained? If the metaphor is to bear doctrinal fruit, it should yield at least some intelligence of the mode and process. The picture of two wrestlers or duelists is hardly congruous when spirits are in conflict. If quanta of spiritual "energy" may be thought of, perhaps, in the case of creatures, how can God fight against creatures, even high-ranking ones? There is no common measure between his infinite power—one of his names is Pantokratōr, Master of all—and the devil's limited power; the fact that the devil can act only on God's sovereign permission (Job!) highlights this radical breach of symmetry.

The difficulty is compounded by the biblical emphasis on the cross of Jesus as the locus and means of victory. We can easily understand victory when bigger battalions crush weaker troops (King Frederick of Prussia is reported to have said that God is on the side of big battalions), but the balance of forces at Calvary looks somewhat different. How can this dying man be proclaimed the victor?

The notion of power looks deceptively simple. But what is spiritual power? And what is its relationship with ethics? If the whole truth of atonement is sufficiently expressed in terms of God overpowering Satan, what about the demands of justice and holiness as they confront sinful and unclean people? These questions suggest that polemic language is both effective and biblical when preaching the effect of the atonement, but to understand (in part) what took place at Calvary, we must inquire both further and deeper into scriptural complexity.

The Paradoxical Way of Divine Victory

How does the Lamb wage his war? In a way well adapted to the enemy's forces—a primary requirement in any kind of war!

But what are these forces? In Scripture, the negative powers that have arisen against the Lord God and against the goodness of his creation, the evil factors that hold men in slavery, are called the devil's cobelligerents, sin and death, the flesh and the world (at least in some contexts). When polemic language is used, however, for God's and Christ's dealings with sin, death, flesh, and world, one cannot miss the literary (or rhetorical) device of personification. Only Satan and *archai*, principalities, in the heavenlies are persons or quasi persons. Inasmuch as the paradigm of warfare suits God's dealings with them, we will concentrate on the way the power of Satan and his troops is established through temptation and accusation—without forgetting the link with sin, death, and so on. This will be the first stage in this brief inquiry. The second stage scrutinizes the biblical data concerning the fight itself and the divine victory.

The Power of Temptation

In canonical order, the first manifestation of Satan's activity is *seductive temptation*. This presupposes that we wisely follow the New Testament (2 Cor. 11:3; Rev. 12:9; 20:2) and identify the "original *(archaios)* serpent" as the devil.[35] Undoubtedly, "Tempter" is an important title of the devil (Matt. 4:3; 1 Thess. 3:5); it was the devil's success in the first temptation that ensured him a continuing sway over humankind. His ability to lead men and women astray and to make them so unlike their Creator, so ungodly, is a major aspect of his efficacy as the enemy of God and God's holy law.

The basis of this efficacy is deception. Only when human beings accept a distorted view of reality can they choose and travel the way of their own death. (This is the biblical approximation of the Socratic "Nobody does wrong *[akousiōs]* willingly.") Satan as the Tempter is the "father of lies" (John 8:44); he works with *methodeia* (Eph. 4:14), "insidious wiles" according to Clinton Arnold;[36] he catches people alive in his "snares" (2 Tim. 2:26). Since being is of God, he can only manipulate the *praestigia*, artifices, of mere appearance (cf. the third temptation of Christ in Matt.

35. I have argued elsewhere that sober interpretation would result in this conclusion on the basis of the Old Testament and its context.
36. Arnold, *Ephesians*, 118.

4:8, or the way he disguises himself in 2 Cor. 11:14–15). Note-worthy in this connection is the destructive impact of false doc-trine in the churches. The devil's supreme agents among men seem to be the *Antichrists* who twist the confession and teach a sham version of Christianity: They keep the outward form of godliness while denying what gives it strength (2 Tim. 3:5; 1 John 2:18–27). The dragon's chosen representative in Revelation, the Beast, is a parody of Christ, a deceptive imitation.

The Tempter's power is reinforced by the developments in human nature and human society. Once one has yielded to temp-tation, the force of human habit (in itself a useful, precious "mechanism" of creation) works in favor of further sinning. Be-lieving the lie further blinds individuals who can no longer rec-ognize the true shape of things. Sin settles in and produces that law in our members that frustrates the wishes of our consciences (Rom. 7:23)—the "flesh" as an associate of the devil and a dimen-sion of our bondage. And then human solidarity, the mimetic im-pulse (which Aristotle noticed and René Girard uses as the cor-nerstone of his system),[37] gives sinful behavior a contagious power. The lies of seduction, to which the lies of self-justification

37. Girard, a French scholar whose career developed in the United States, has brought forward revolutionary insights regarding the genesis of culture, with a striking celebration of biblical uniqueness. His several books (e.g., *Des choses cachées depuis la fondation du monde* [Paris: Grasset, 1978]) strike the same note: In the beginning was the most powerful impulse that pushes men to imi-tate one another; contrary to common stereotypes, this does not lead to harmo-ny but to escalating violence. Imitators become rivals; they claim the same goods and retaliate endlessly. The mimetic crisis must have led to the destruction of many early human groups, but sometimes the unleashed violence of all was at-tracted by the slightly different individual in the group (e.g., an albino man), and he became the scapegoat for the community. Since the murder of the one ex-hausted the violence of all, peace was restored, extraordinarily, and the group was saved. A twofold conclusion was drawn: First, the man must have been *guilty*, and, second, he must have been *divine* for such mighty effects to be born from his death. Such was the matrix of all institutions and, especially, of *sacri-fice*, for the group decided to reenact, in attenuated form, the marvelous solution that had saved its life, with a sacred substitute slain on behalf of the community. Only in the Bible is the murder of the innocent man unveiled as such and con-demned; only in the Bible, therefore, is sacrificial thinking rejected. Girard has to grant that the Old Testament has not reached purity on this topic, but he claims that the New Testament does *not* view Jesus' death as a sacrifice—except for the Epistle to the Hebrews, which he discards accordingly.

are soon combined (for conscience cannot be totally muffled), grow into the symbolic system of a culture, which molds the mind of every member from childhood onward. Groups behave like proud and cruel bandits and succeed in enlisting even the noblest of passions (humility, sacrificial devotion) in the service of oppressive or idolatrous ends. Such is the "world," whose friendship is enmity toward God (James 4:4) and which "lies in the evil one" (1 John 5:19) or under Satan as *archōn* (John 12:31).

Is Satan the *Afflicter* another face of Satan the Tempter? One cannot be dogmatic, yet the double meaning of *peirasmos*, temptation and trial, tends to suggest this is the case. In both cases the devil induces to sin: in seduction he draws; through affliction he presses. Many afflictions result from actions that have been inspired by the devil as Tempter: either the self-destructive consequences of a person's own transgressions or the effects of the work of evildoers in aggression, dishonesty, persecution. If subjection to sickness is part of the tyranny of the devil (*katadynasteuomenous*, oppressed, Acts 10:38), this fact may be interpreted as a global consequence of sin's entry into the world upon the serpent's instigation (Genesis 3; Rom. 5:12; 8:20). The power of affliction still stems from the power of temptation.

The topic of demonization is too complex for treatment here,[38] but it is permissible to consider this exercise of satanic power, though clearly distinct, as a higher degree and a stronger kind of influence—temptation "cubed." The Book of Job represents Satan as able to unleash thunderbolts and cyclonic winds (Job 1:16, 19), thus wielding powers not issuing from temptation. Such action, however, is exceptional in Scripture. Satan is not in view when one reads about storms in the Gospels. It would be unwise, therefore, to raise the theme of his ability to use elements of nature to major importance in the analysis of his power, apart from his activity as the Tempter.

An affirmation that the devil gains power through temptation reveals two observations: It cannot be the last secret of his sway over

---

38. The crippled woman in Luke 13:10–16, whom Satan had bound for eighteen years (v. 16), was *not* demon possessed but only suffered from infirmity; there is no exorcism. Jesus lays his hands on her, and the "spirit" she has "had" (it may mean "disposition") is "of infirmity" *(pneuma echousa astheneias)*. The case, then, could be "borderline" between the universal Acts 10:38 oppression and particular demonization.

humankind, and it cannot help us significantly to understand why God had to fight to break that sway and how he did it in Christ.

Temptation is suggestion. It requires, in order to succeed, to find what it cannot create: the formally free consent of the human person. The first temptation was purely from the outside, and there was no reason or compulsion to augment its power. Adam freely sinned, and this is why Paul stressed the role of the man: "Through a man sin entered the world" (Rom. 5:12).[39] Temptations, since, still require the self-determination of human will to give birth to sin. (Even in the case of demonization, constraint was preceded by choice and is still accompanied by choice.)

Scripture reveals that Satan does not act independently of God when he tempts or tries the children of men. The Lord's permissive decree lies behind and above whatever the devil as Tempter can do. This accounts for the strange substitution of Satan for the Lord as the one who incited King David to sin in 1 Chronicles 21:1 as compared with 2 Samuel 24:1. Chronicles makes explicit that YHWH (as a righteous judge of Israel's sins) decreed to allow Satan to tempt David; Satan did the tempting, but he was fulfilling the divine purpose. The Book of Job, again, illustrates the same principle in the case of afflictions: Satan acts only on God's permission. How, then, can there be such a fight between the two?

The Power of Accusation

The other title of Satan is the *Accuser,* as he is called in the most polemic passage, Revelation 12:10. This is the basic meaning of the more usual name Satan.[40] *Śāṭān* is a word for the adversary. In the law court, as in Psalm 109:6, the corresponding verb *śāṭan* means to stand against someone and to accuse him or her. In Zechariah's night-vision (chap. 3), *the* Satan stands before the divine judge to accuse, *śāṭan,* Joshua the high priest, on whom all the uncleanness accumulated through seventy years without atoning sacrifices has been laid. Satan's role is that of the public prosecutor. He is also the accuser in Job 1.

Although less precise, the Greek translation *diabolos* retains this meaning, and Peter, for instance, remembers the judicial

39. An interesting contrast with Wisdom 2:24: "Through the Devil's envy, death entered the world."
40. So Hamilton settles in "Satan," 986.

connotations (1 Peter 5:8, *antidikos,* adversary in court). In Luke 22:31, reminiscent of Job, Satan's aim in "sifting" the apostles is probably to charge them with unworthiness and inadequacy before God. "Jesus, however," writes Victor Hamilton, "is Peter's advocate (Luke 22:32) pleading against Satan the accuser."[41] Candidates to the overseers' offices must not be recent converts, for the devil is on watch to catch them slipping and to bring on them a judgment *(krima)* of condemnation (1 Tim. 3:6).

How is Satan's role as the Accuser related to his *power?* If Satan's opposition to the Lord were a matter of mere power, the rebel's finite resources would equal zero confronted with infinity. But the Accuser can appeal to justice. He may also indulge in slander, but his force resides in the rightness of his accusation. Joshua *is* unclean, unspeakably unclean (*ṣôʾîm,* Zech. 3:4). The righteous Judge of all the earth, who can do only right, cannot refuse to hear the charges the Accuser brings without denying himself. In other words, the weapon in the devil's hand is God's own law, God's holy and perfect law—hence the association in some passages of the law and inimical powers, which Aulén was not able to read aright.

In this light, we may interpret the statement in Hebrews that the devil holds the power *(kratos)* of death (2:14). Throughout Scripture, death appears as the punishment *God* brings down upon sinners; it is YHWH who causes death and makes alive (1 Sam. 2:6). The devil holds the power inasmuch as he seduces into deadly ways those who lack judgment (Prov. 8:36; 9:18), and he secures their condemnation as the prosecutor of humankind. Using the force of law, he demands successfully that they die. In the last analysis, the fear of death, the means of human bondage (Heb. 2:15), is the fear of condemnation. Because men and women dread the unknown judgment, they do not turn to God for mercy. They desperately grab elements of this world for illusory protection and become the slaves of idols. They stand helpless under the influence of the devil.

The separation between God and his image-creatures, as required by the accusation based on divine law, appears to be the deepest factor in the human plight. God will have no fellowship with criminals who still overflow with and are covered by the filth of their crimes. Hence the slavery of the "flesh." There is

41. Ibid., 989.

no source of energy within a person to counteract the anarchy of impulses and habits of wrongdoing. Hence the slavery of the "world." As the "sense of deity" is deprived of its true object, it falls back on poor and weak substitutes.

The radical vacancy at the innermost root of personality—God *interior intimo meo*[42]—explains that even the formal freedom that consents to evil amounts to a sort of actual, "material" bondage. Whereas temptation comes from the outside, God's presence is essential (in the strongest sense of this word) *within* freedom, so that his judicial withdrawal in the presence of unsolved guilt affects freedom itself, and human beings become *slaves* of sin, flesh, world, and devil. This seems to be the apostle's thought as he declares, "The power *[dynamis]* of sin is the law" (1 Cor. 15:56). The law of God, precisely because it is good and holy, separates us, condemned sinners, from our good and holy God, and we fall prey to agencies of wickedness.

Satan's major weapon, as he enforces his rule, is thus divine law and justice. He is the relentless Accuser, day and night.

Victory through Obedience in Truth

If Satan's sway is established through temptation first—using deceit and twisted interpretations of God's Word, playing on the influence of the "flesh" and the "world"—and more deeply through the validity of the accusation he can bring against us as he appeals to God's own holy commandment, how could it be overthrown? Scripture witnesses to a strategy that shows a remarkable symmetry with what we just analyzed. Against the Tempter-Liar, Jesus is raised as the Teacher of Truth who calls us back to cordial obedience. Much more: He *exemplifies* total obedience to the Word of the Father, from beginning to end, to the death of crucifixion, and he thus opens the way for his disciples to follow him. Even more deeply, against the Accuser, Jesus is raised as the Lamb of God who achieves the satisfaction of all legal claims by taking upon himself the sin of the world and thus doing away with all condemnation. The devil stands "disarmed," and the floodgates of the life-giving Spirit may open. This and the next section briefly survey the New

42. Saint Augustine, *Confessions*, III.vi.11 ("more interior than the innerest part of me").

Testament attestation along those two main avenues: against the Tempter, obedience in truth; against the Accuser, vicarious punishment, the ground of free justification.

"If you abide in my word, you are truly my disciples; you shall know the truth and the truth shall make you free" (John 8:31–32, author's translation). Jesus ascribes liberation to the truth of his Word, liberation from the tyranny of sin (v. 34) and the devil, the father of lies (v. 44). Since reception of the truth equals *obedience* to the truth, according to New Testament perspectives (e.g., 1 Peter 1:22; Rom. 6:17, which identifies the truth of the Word as the "model of doctrine"), and since obedience is precisely what temptation sets out to dissolve, obedience in the light of revealed truth seems to define the way of victory—victory over the Tempter and his network of deception. To fight against the most pernicious of the devil's inventions, those of the Antichrist, Scripture repeatedly calls for unfailing attachment to the truth that was taught "in the beginning" and the keeping of the Lord's commandments. The "young men" are able to defeat the evil one by the strength of the Word of God abiding in them (1 John 2:14).

A confirmation that the Tempter has to yield before obedience and the testimony of truth is found in the account of Jesus' threefold temptation, the test he underwent for qualification at the start of his official ministry. Jesus frustrated the devil's plans by his strict submission to his Father's will and by unmasking the devil's distortion of the truth—citing the Word and applying more rigorous hermeneutics to it. We should not underestimate the importance of this preliminary fight in the desert for the victory of our salvation, which Dietrich Bonhoeffer magnified. If Jesus had accepted any of the devil's proposals, we would be lost forever.

Yet this was only the first round (as Luke 4:13 intimates: *achri kairou,* until a time [of opportunity]). It is unlikely that the parable of the strong man bound (Mark 3:27) alludes to Jesus' act of overcoming the threefold temptation. Rather, Jesus' ministry of deliverance *anticipates* the victory through which the prince of this world will be cast down (John 12:31; Luke 10:18, a vision of the future accomplishment of Christ's victory). The entire burden of biblical teaching ties the devil's defeat to the supreme event of Christ's death and resurrection. Matthew 4:1–11 (and parallels) demonstrates that Jesus was fit for the fight.

The role of obedience and truth is by no means negligible in the supreme event. Christ was obedient unto death, the death of the cross (Phil. 2:8). Consequently, he was raised to glory. The spiritual struggle of Gethsemane highlights the place of that total submission. As he answered Pilate in his "beautiful confession" (1 Tim. 6:13), Jesus testified to the truth (John 18:37). Nowhere is the truth more powerfully manifested than at the cross and in the resurrection light: the truth of the heinousness of human sin, the truth of the objective weight of human guilt, the truth of God's sovereignty, the truth of God's infinite mercy and love. We may and must retain, therefore, obedience in truth as a partial answer to the question we have raised, but since the power of the Tempter-Liar is not the decisive dimension of his domination, we must investigate even further.

Victory through Vicarious Punishment

One of the few passages that deal explicitly with the way of Christ's victory over our spiritual foes—maybe the most explicit of all—paradoxically connects his triumph to the cross and precisely to the cancellation of the bond of our debt (as defined by the ordinances of the law) when Jesus was crucified (Col. 2:14–15). Then and there were the principalities and powers, the chief of whom is called Satan, "disarmed."[43] The action concerns judicial claims. Since God can be expected to uphold the

43. This is the more common understanding of the clause *apekdysamenos tas archas kai tas exousias*, "having divested [of their power or weapons] the principalities and the authorities," and it is best argued for by F. F. Bruce in *The Epistles to the Colossians, to Philemon, and to the Ephesians*, New International Commentary on the New Testament (Grand Rapids: Eerdmans, 1984, 1993), 107, with a full note, n. 82, on the various interpretations of the words. Other renderings have been proposed: that of most Greek fathers (Christ "stripping off the hostile powers from himself") has little to commend it; that of the Latin fathers, who connect the words *archas* and *exousias* with the last clause in the sentence (Christ "stripped himself [of his body of flesh] and publicly exposed the principalities and powers"), would be much preferable. (It is also found in the Peshitto-Syriac version.) Those who advocate interpretations other than Bruce's argue from the use of the *middle* voice in the verbal participle *apekdysamenos*, having divested or stripped off—from himself, they say. But it better suits the wording to interpret the middle voice as "simply indicat[ing] the personal interest of the subject in the action of the verb" (Bruce, 107), as Hellenistic usage fully allows, and thus to retain the more common understanding. In that case, the text explicitly teaches that the demonic powers were divested of their power, disarmed, by the cancellation of the legal debt on the cross.

rules he has set, we can also expect that the cancellation was obtained through the payment of the legal debt. This appears to be confirmed by the many *ransom* sayings that state that the life or blood of Christ *was the price paid* to free human beings from bondage. (Galatians 3:23 indicates that we were imprisoned by the law, *hypo nomon ephrouroumetha sunkleiomenoi;* we were locked up, as in prison, under the law.) Efforts to elude the thought that justice was satisfied, and thus the bond that was against us removed, look strangely artificial.[44] F. F. Bruce aptly summarizes the meaning for believers: "Not only has he [Christ] blotted out the record of their indebtedness but he has subjugated those powers whose possession of the damning indictment was a means of controlling them."[45]

Revelation 12 reflects the same understanding. How have the brothers overcome the devil and his host? Not by superior might but "by the blood of the Lamb" (Rev. 12:11). Satan was the Accuser, and he prevailed as long as he could point to their sins. But the blood of the Lamb was the price paid for the cancellation of their debt. The blood of the Lamb wiped out the guilt of their sins forever, and the devil was disarmed. Similarly, Hebrews 2:14 stresses that Jesus deprived the devil of his power *(katargēsē)* through his death, and we are told that "he has died as a ransom to set them [those who are called] free from the sins committed under the first covenant" (Heb. 9:15), his blood obtaining the remission of their sins (Heb.

44. Is this Daniel G. Reid's thought? In his article "Triumph," in *Dictionary of Paul and His Letters,* 949, he writes: "We may conceive Paul's thinking as follows: The powers unleashed their assault on Christ's body, in a climactic expression of the nations attacking Zion, and on the cross they destroyed his 'body of flesh' (Col 2:11; cf. Scott, 34–35). But this was a pyrrhic victory. Christ absorbed and exhausted their fury in his death (with his vindication in the resurrection implied) and so he triumphed over the powers (Col. 2:15)." This attempt eclipses the judicial orientation of verse 14. It appears to rely on the metaphor of "absorption," for which there is scant evidence in the language of the Bible: When a physical or "chemical" metaphor is used, it is that of removing, wiping away, or covering, not absorbing. "Bearing" or "carrying" sin belongs, as a technical phrase, to the language of justice and means that the appropriate punishment is inflicted. The metaphor of absorption offers little help in the search for some intelligence of what happened. I fail to see why Jesus' death should have absorbed and exhausted the fury of the powers.

45. Bruce, *Epistles,* 110. Bruce quotes Krishna Pal's poetry: "Jesus for thee a body takes, / Thy guilt assumes, thy fetter breaks, / Discharging all thy dreadful debt— / And canst thou then such love forget?"

9:22; cf. 27–28). Already in Zechariah 3, the Lord's rebuke of Satan, based on God's electing grace (v. 2), is not an act of sheer power.[46] It is conjoined with the removal of sin (v. 4), and the angel of the Lord is mentioned as though he had a special role to play in this connection (v. 5). The entire scene is "symbolic of things to come" (v. 8). When the Servant, the Branch, comes, there will be a unique day of atonement efficacious for all ages: "I will remove the guilt *['āwôn]* of this earth [land] in a single day" (v. 9, author's translation). Thus shall Satan be rebuked, at last vanquished.

Satan is not specifically mentioned in Romans 7–8, but the tyranny of the flesh, which checks all wishes of goodness and thwarts the influence of the divine law, is a close association of the devil's power. It is significant, therefore, that Paul does not begin his outline of Christian liberation with the gift of the Spirit (Rom. 8:2) but with a proclamation of perfect justification: "There is now no condemnation" (8:1). Before life-giving fellowship with God could be established, guilt had to be removed, condemnation lifted, accusation silenced, the claims of the law satisfied (for the power of sin is the law). And this happened on the cross: God *condemned* sin in the flesh (8:3). In the person of the substitute, who came in the *likeness* of sinful flesh (solidarity but sinlessness), sin transferred was indeed condemned and the death sentence executed.[47] Substitu-

---

46. See my "Zacharie 3. Josué et le Grand Jour des Expiations," *Etudes Théologiques et Religieuses* 54 (1079): 264–70.

47. In "Triumph," 950, Reid again looks for another meaning. He explains: "The Son entered sin's sphere of dominion. But when sin pressed its claim upon Christ, he, being guiltless, condemned sin in the flesh." This is hardly persuasive; there is no warrant in the passage for the idea of a claim pressed, and Christ's guiltlessness does not amount to God's condemnation of sin in the flesh. Reid does not consider the possibility that *peri hamartias* means "as a sin offering" (so NIV). William Sanday and Arthur C. Headlam, *A Critical and Exegetical Commentary on the Epistle to the Romans*, International Critical Commentary, 5th ed. (Edinburgh: T & T Clark, 1907), 193, already observed: "The parallel passage, vi. 6–11, shows that this summary condemnation of Sin takes place in the Death of Christ, and not in His Life." Reid's comment on Galatians 3:13 also follows a rather circuitous route. As he introduces a reference to the fate of Canaanite kings in Joshua (of which there is not the slightest reminiscence in the chapter!), he explains: "In a reversal of that imagery, Paul speaks of Christ absorbing the curse, or *ḥērem*, of the divine warrior against Israel, and so bringing redemption for his people and in turn for the world" (951). We encounter the metaphor of absorbing and a doubtful identification of *ḥērem* and curse.

tion under the legal punishment is the foundation of victorious liberation.

Revelation 5 unfolds in symbolic picture the paradox of Christ as victor and victim and the true connection between the two. How did the Lion of Judah, the apocalyptic seven-horned Lamb, triumph? He was slain and purchased with his blood people from every nation (vv. 6, 9). The Servant Lamb, the sacrificial victim, who bore our sins at the cost of his life, was able to cast down the Accuser. *Agnus Victor*. Most likely, this was already the association in the John 1:29 greeting: The victorious Lamb of God takes away *(airei)* the sin of the world as he takes it upon himself *(airei)*.[48]

The Treasure of the Church

The discernment that the proclamation of *Christus Victor* should not replace the gospel of his vicarious punishment and atoning sacrifice but should be seen as flowing from this central mystery is no twenty-first-century novelty. Our debt to the major sixteenth-century Reformers constrains us to show that Martin Luther and John Calvin had clear insight into that connection.

Luther not only maintained propitiation and satisfaction, as already shown, but also taught the relationship between them and the devil's defeat. Paul Althaus summarizes Luther's view: "The satisfaction that God's justice demands is the primary and decisive meaning of Christ's work, in particular of his death. All the rest hangs on this, the Powers spoiled of all right and power."[49] After he stressed that Christ had to die as a satisfaction, Luther added: Christ "reached his priesthood through his death and his kingdom through his priesthood,"[50] his kingdom (and kingship) implying his triumph over the enemy.

48. The weakness in Dodd's interpretation is his treatment of the phrase, as Leon Morris shows in *The Apostolic Preaching of the Cross* (London: Tyndale, 1955), 138f.

49. Althaus, *Die Theologie Martin Luthers*, 193, as quoted in Eißler, "Die Heilstat Jesu Christi," 128.

50. Weimar Ausgabe 10 I/1, 721:2, as quoted in Althaus, *Die Theologie Martin Luthers* (his 194), quoted in n. 42, explains that, for Luther, Christ is victor of hell, death, and devil in his capacity as King. "The priestly ministry is the foundation and the vehicle of the royal ministry, because hell, death and Devil are a threat for man only because of God's wrath."

Calvin's emphasis on penal substitution cannot be doubted. Yet he also preached vigorously Christ's victory over the devil and his agents. Did he clarify how they were related? Calvin explained the Hebrews 2:15 liberation with the clause, "when, by sustaining our curse, he [Christ] took out what was dreadful in death."[51] In regard to Colossians 2:15, he wrote "that they [the hostile powers] are disarmed, so that they can bring nothing against us, since the certificate of our guilt was itself cancelled,"[52] and, for him, it was cancelled by adequate payment. In his seventh sermon on the passion, he stated, "Jesus Christ triumphed on the cross. It is true that [St. Paul] applies this to the fact that he tore up the obligation that was against us, and that he acquitted us towards God, and that by that means Satan was defeated."[53]

The key position of the doctrine of vicarious punishment answers to the privilege of personal-relational-juridical categories, within the framework of covenant, to deal with the divine-human communication, over against that of ontological participation and moral assimilation in other strands of the Christian tradition. This "mind" is biblical. However, such a position does not make other languages and schemes superfluous, and it does not rule out ontological dimensions and moral influence. The polemic presentation, especially, is a welcome complement: When one understands that Christ's victory was based on his sacrifice, one should unfold the fruit of his death as radical and universal victory! Understanding that Satan was defeated as the Accuser may help us to retain the particle of truth in the awkward suggestion that God's attributes of mercy and justice had to be "reconciled" by the cross: Though God's attributes are one (descriptions of the one essence), once evil entered the world (through God's wholly mysterious, inscrutable permission), his justice became in a way the enemy's weapon—until the divine wisdom (and love) provided the way for God to be both just and the one who justifies sinners through faith in Jesus (Rom. 3:26).

The mystery of Christ's punishment as the head for his body, as the shepherd for his sheep, in free and yet lawful substitution, which resulted in his victory over the Tempter and Ac-

51. *Calvini opera* LV:33.
52. Ibid., LII:109.
53. Ibid., XLVI:918.

cuser, is the core treasure of the deposit of Scripture truth in the church. Let no one rob us of our assurance. Let us paradoxically proclaim *Christus Victor* as the *Agnus* that was slain. Let us boldly unfold the cosmic and metacosmic fruitfulness of his atoning and substitutionary sacrifice as victory over evil and over the evil one. And let us draw the existential and ethical consequences of the way of the Lamb: *Vicit agnus noster; eum sequamur* (Our lamb has conquered; let us follow him).

Part 2
Expanding Particular Zones

4

What Is *This Life* For?

Expanding Our View of Salvation

VINCENT BACOTE

How is salvation understood from the perspective of communities with significant legacies of oppression and victimization? There are numerous approaches to this question, though most come by way of the path of liberation theology. This chapter takes a different path, seeking to help evangelicals understand salvation in a fashion that is broader than the important aspect of the eternal destiny of individual souls. Rather than attempting to present an encyclopedic view of this matter, I will discuss the experiences of certain groups and offer an approach to soteriology that focuses on *one* element, namely, the meaning and implications of God's salvific work in Christ for life on this side of eternity. I will first expose what I perceive to be inadequacies in evangelical soteriology; then I will express some ways that oppressed groups may perceive soteriology; finally, I will present four aspects of what I call "concrete soteriology."

At the start, it is necessary to make two comments concerning perspectives on salvation that come from "the margins." First, an "us versus them" dualism often emerges in discourse concerning oppressed groups. I do not write with the assumption that anyone is sinless nor that the oppressed are redeemed by virtue of victimization. That said, my focus does require speaking from minority perspectives, and the language used conveys sympathy for the communities considered here—although sympathy does not mean a free pass for some and a blanket condemnation for others.

Second, while postmodernity has rightly awakened many to the reality of the "other," the awareness of differing perspectives can intentionally or unintentionally result in marginalization. One reason for this is that some celebrate the articulation of previously silent or muffled voices and then proceed to protect the existence of such perspectives by labeling the discourse a unique form of language that can be understood only by the "tribe" or those who possess a sympathetic ear. In such a case, the celebration is limited to a particular group, and though there may be room in academic or political discourse for the group, the insights gained serve only the group itself and fail to benefit the larger populace. Marginalization can also occur when the privatized, individualistic faith characteristic of much of contemporary Western Christianity (whether more liberal or conservative) renders such perspectives "just one more available option" on the theological buffet. The voices from the margin are marginalized because other Christians, who are happy that "someone is out there talking about these things and taking up a long-neglected cause," applaud the arrival of the voices, welcome them to the buffet, and subsequently ignore their contribution. While we may be happy that "they" have finally raised their voices, our only comment may be that it is "good for *them*." It is my hope that what I offer will be considered carefully as good for all of us, not as a cause for an empty celebration that merely transports these perspectives from one margin to another. To put it differently, we need a kind of ecumenism in which there is neither uncritical acceptance of new voices nor renewed competition to see which perspective should gain dominance in our era. I agree with Justo Gonzàlez, who says, "On the contrary, what we seek, jointly

with all others who are speaking the words of the new reformation, is to call the entire church to obedience, and to bring
whatever insight we may have to the theological task of the
church as a whole."[1]

I chose the title "What Is *This Life* For?" as I reflected on my
assignment, which was to consider how salvation might be understood by those who are oppressed and marginalized in society and what one thing I would like to say to evangelicals about
the subject. In my reflection, I became aware of the fact that the
soteriological emphasis can go in one of two distinct directions
when existence itself is a constant crisis. One emphasis is ex-
treme otherworldliness. Salvation is literally an escape from
this life, and it may serve as a coping mechanism. In this case,
Christianity is indeed an opiate for the masses, a transcendent
drug that transports the oppressed to another reality, to an al-
tered consciousness. The second emphasis is the exact opposite: Salvation takes on a very concrete character and is a matter of physical deliverance that contains a spiritual element.
This latter emphasis is more characteristic of oppressed and
marginalized communities. When they raise questions about
salvation, they do not wonder merely whether they will ultimately live with God forever "on the other side"; they wonder
when and how God will sustain them and ultimately rescue
them from their plight in the here and now. When they consider
categories such as sin, grace, atonement, and sanctification,
there is little space for the abstract. Instead, much attention is
given to the details of life *now*.

Soteriological Inadequacy in Evangelical Theology?

Evangelical soteriology has rightly focused on the salvation of individual souls, for the eternal destiny of individuals is indeed a central aspect of the gospel. But it is not the only aspect. In fairness, the
variety of traditions that comprise the evangelical heritage have not
always magnified the soul-saving aspect of salvation in ways that
minimized the significance of salvation for the details of earthly ex-

1. Justo Gonzàlez, *Mañana: Christian Theology from a Hispanic Perspective*
(Nashville: Abingdon, 1990), 53.

istence. Prior to the twentieth century, there was considerable evangelical engagement in all areas of life. In particular, those who held a postmillennial eschatology sought to transform society so that the kingdom of God would eventually appear on earth. Causes such as temperance and abolition are noteworthy examples of the attempts to save both souls and society. Between 1900 and 1930, however, a shift that some scholars have labeled the "great reversal"[2] led to a distinct de-emphasis on matters of social concern. This reversal was a reaction to the social gospel of liberalism and the result of a shift to a rapture-focused premillennialism as the dominant view of eschatology. Concerned that the gospel message of eternal life through Christ's atoning work would be lost in a sea of social concern and convinced that the Bible teaches that society will only deteriorate, fundamentalists and evangelicals directed their soteriological gaze toward eternal matters. Their approach to discipleship centered on spiritual disciplines that focused on the inner life so that one could be "ready" when Jesus makes his sudden and invisible return to rapture the church.[3]

While the events of the era make this shift somewhat understandable, there is much to lament, particularly from the per-

2. See David O. Moberg, *The Great Reversal: Evangelicalism versus Social Concern* (Philadelphia: Lippincott, 1972), particularly 28–43; Donald Dayton, *Discovering an Evangelical Heritage* (New York: Harper & Row, 1976), 121–37; and George Marsden, *Fundamentalism and American Culture* (New York: Oxford University Press, 1980), 85–93. A different interpretation of this reversal is found in Kathryn Teresa Long, *The Revival of 1857–58: Interpreting an American Religious Awakening* (New York: Oxford University Press, 1998). Long argues that the revival of 1857–58 focused on inward piety rather than social change and that at the very least the seeds of the great reversal were already present because the social action oriented form of response to revival was actually deemphasized. This was followed by events such as the Civil War, the rising influence of Brethren piety (more focused on a longing for one's heavenly home), and the revivals and crusade evangelism associated with Dwight L. Moody, creating even then a drift from soteriology that focuses on living for God "here."

3. This is not to say that no one focused on the inner life prior to the great reversal. The point is that the emphasis on salvation and awaiting the rapture led to an emphasis on the inner life that made one's faith such a "heart" matter that it was privatized and not public in any way that would confront or transform the existing social order. It should also be noted that fundamentalists and evangelicals who were amillennial or postmillennial (definitely a sizeable minority) did not do a great deal to transform the society in ways that emphasized justice for the oppressed.

spective of socially and economically disadvantaged segments of the population. The civil rights struggle is ample evidence of the lamentable character of an exclusively soul-saving approach to soteriology. The most disturbing trait of this approach to salvation is that salvation seems powerless to transform the deep-seated racial pathology in the United States. Among the most noteworthy and revealing comments to this effect comes from E. J. Carnell, who wrote:

> I find it easy to be patient with Billy Graham. Though I have been preaching for many years, I have never devoted an entire sermon to the sins of the white man, and the chief reason for this failure is my failure to find a way to measure and defeat racial pride in my own life. It is not easy to preach against oneself. Ministers expose the sins of the laity with great passion and eloquence, but they seldom expose the sins of ministers. The tragedy is that our desire to actuate the law of love is not matched by the wisdom and virtue needed to succeed. If we pass real estate zoning laws, we do an injustice to the Negro. But if we let the Negro buy a house in a fashionable suburb, we do an injustice to vested property interest. With rare exceptions, real estate values are certain to plunge.[4]

Carnell's words, while admirable for their candor, raise questions about his evangelical soteriology as well as his homiletics, as they make one wonder what other personal sins he refused to preach against. While he admits that he has difficulties overcoming his own internal struggles, his comments also reveal a blindness to the gravity of social and structural sin. It is as if one shares the sentiment that racial injustice is evil yet lacks the theological vision and transformative power to see the need for and a strategy to frame a necessary revolution. Carnell's soul-saving soteriology produces sentiment and possibly even anguish about the plight of oppressed people, but it is not adequately equipped to do much more than lament and mourn the terrible plight of "those people." There is a clear concern to "conserve" the status quo out of fear that the actions for justice may yield too much concomitant injustice. Ap-

4. E. J. Carnell, *The Case for Biblical Christianity,* ed. Ronald Nash (Grand Rapids: Eerdmans, 1969), 90–91.

parently this gospel does not produce adequate wisdom for confronting deep-seated social pathology. If that is the case, is it really the gospel?

There are evangelicals who will ask, "But what about all the well-meaning Christians who argue that the only way society can change is one saved soul at a time?" The question itself reveals an exclusively individualistic conception of salvation that neglects the reality of corporate and structural sin. It is true that revolutionary changes occur in the hearts of converted Christians, but how often does the revolution manifest itself in ways that go beyond the inner life? History is full of regenerate segregationists, slaveholders, and even Nazis! They claimed to have had changed hearts, but they were also committed to social structures that validated oppression. We might find such people outrageous, but were they all that far from Carnell in their soteriology?

If one adds to the equation the eschatological emphasis characteristic of much popular evangelicalism in the twentieth century, one recognizes that a soul-saving soteriology so emphasizes getting to heaven before the rapture that adherents do not value directing time and energy to causes that are not explicitly committed to evangelism or spiritually focused discipleship. Struggles such as civil rights may be good things, but they are not nearly as important as winning souls.

Soteriological Visions

One interesting motif that has been used by many oppressed groups is the exodus. The exodus serves as a dominant liberation motif for various forms of liberation theology, and it is indeed helpful. I would like to take a cue from Robert Allen Warrior, however, and use the Canaanite experience as a motif. In his chapter titled "A Native American Perspective: Canaanites, Cowboys, and Indians," Warrior challenges the use of the exodus story as a universal model for liberation across all contexts and oppressed groups. He says:

> As a member of the Osage Nation of American Indians who stands in solidarity with other tribal people around the world, I read the Exodus stories with Canaanite eyes. And, it is the Canaan-

ite story that has been overlooked by those seeking to articulate theologies of liberation. . . . The Conquest stories, with all their violence and injustice, must be taken seriously by those who believe in the god of the Old Testament. Commentaries and critical works rarely mention these texts. When they do, they express little concern for the indigenes and their rights as human beings and as nations. The same blindness is evident in theologies that use the Exodus motif as their basis for political action. The leading into the land becomes just one more redemptive moment rather than a violation of innocent people's rights to land and self-determination.[5]

This disturbing passage points to the experience of Christians who have been oppressed by other Christians. Oppression was certainly the case in America, where the indigenous people, whether converted or not, were nearly wiped out, placed on reservations, and subjected to harsh discrimination by people who saw themselves as Christians. It is not too strong to say that the traumatic experiences of this group place them more in the category of Canaanite than of Israelite, at least by virtue of their experience.

Is there an insight or helpful soteriological point here? Warrior puts us on an interesting path by noting the terms of the covenant found in Exodus 20–23 and Deuteronomy 7–9:

> The god who delivered Israel from slavery will lead the people into the land and keep them there as long as they live up to the terms of the covenant: "You shall not wrong a stranger or oppress him, for you were strangers in the land of Egypt. You shall not afflict any widow or orphan. If you do afflict them, and they cry out to me, I will surely hear their cry; and my wrath will burn, and I will kill you with the sword, and your wives shall become widows and your children fatherless" (Exod. 22:21).[6]

Those who entered the Promised Land had restrictions placed on them by God concerning their destruction of humans outside the covenant. The stranger was to be protected, not abused.

5. In *Voices from the Margin: Interpreting the Bible in the Third World*, ed. R. S. Sugirtharajah (Maryknoll, N.Y.: Orbis, 1995), 279, 283.
6. Ibid., 280–81.

I here must register my disagreement with Warrior's interpretation of the passage: It refers to non-Israelites seeking shel-
ter, not to any blatantly idolatrous Gentile whom the Israelites
might encounter. Nevertheless, it is true that Native Americans
suffered at the hands of those who saw America as a Promised
Land of conquest and could more naturally perceive themselves as Canaanites because their land was taken. Yet it is quite
a shift to think that any Christian would identify with the
Canaanites given their negative characterization in the Bible.
Warrior identifies not with the Canaanites' characterization,
however, but with their experience. His perspective is that Native Americans do not perceive themselves as the enemies of
God's people, yet their history is one of conquest similar to that
of the Canaanites as the Israelites took possession of the Promised Land. (Indeed, Puritan settlers used this kind of language,
referring to Native Americans as Canaanites and the New
World as the Promised Land.) For those Native Americans who
are Christian and have something of a Canaanite self-percep-
tion, salvation means far more than a ticket to heaven. It includes a cry for literal deliverance from devastating circumstances. They are the stranger who has been violated, and it
would seem that their hope in a God who is mighty to save reflects hope for a better future on earth.

Warrior is helpful, but he does not take us where we must
go. While his use of the Canaanite motif raises an important
question about the conduct of the covenant people, he treats
the Canaanites as relatively innocent victims. It is important
first to acknowledge that the Canaanites were sinful. It is
equally important to acknowledge that Israel, though the ben-
eficiary of God's covenant promises, failed to live up to the covenant, committed treason with other gods, and subsequently
had their own "Canaanite experience" of the exile and desola-
tion. This should serve as a cause for reflection for any of us
who label ourselves God's people and prompt us to examine
whether there are idols in our midst, whether they are idols of
self (by virtue of one's race, class, nationality, etc.) or of some
other aspect of creation. This is where Warrior's modification
of the blanket use of the exodus motif can help. Often the exodus is used as a deliverance motif that carries the unspoken assumption that the recipients of divine deliverance are innocent

and will remain so in perpetuity. (This is an error similar to that implicit in Warrior's thinking regarding the Canaanites.) There are no sinlessly innocent victims of destruction or recipients of deliverance. As Warrior correctly notes, the exodus is articulated as a redemptive moment, and what follows is ignored.

Contrary to Warrior, I believe the emphasis should be shifted not to the routing of the Canaanites as much as to the failure of Israel to live differently from those removed from the Promised Land. To use the exodus motif with any accuracy requires reflection on the response of God's people post-liberation. By any account, the post-exodus history of Israel is ultimately a story of disappointment and failure. The Israelites did not succeed in avoiding idolatry and unjust practices. Rather than demonstrating to the world what it means to be image-bearers of God, they instead came down with a case of corporate amnesia and by their actions showed that they had forgotten not only that they were required to treat strangers justly but also that they should promote justice among their own people (e.g., see Micah 3). Sadly, the periods of godly rule were the exception. While God held true to his promises, his people did not, and they eventually suffered as a result.

The implications for God's covenant people today are as enormous as ever. Those who have entered into a covenant relationship with God cannot assume that their "saved" status carries no responsibility for their behavior. The legacy of Christian treatment of Native Americans is lamentable and reveals the hubris that can result from misunderstanding our status as covenant people. The exodus, the arrival in a new land, does not provide legitimation for oppressing the stranger, particularly when one's claim on the land is dubious (Who "gave" the land to the settlers?). Today, there is equal gravity for Christian treatment of strangers. Evangelicals who are secure in their eternal destiny cannot assume that grace protects them from the consequences of covenant infidelity in this life. Injustice remains in our midst, and the recipients of injustice, particularly those who are Christians, cry out to God for a salvation that yields concrete benefits in this life as well as a future eternal bliss.

For Christians who currently live in comfort while others suffer, therefore, a question lingers: Will we learn from the history of Israel, or will we repeat the Israelites' folly? Theological reflection and practice require that notions of liberation and use of the exodus story carry with them the responsibility of covenantal faithfulness.

Native Americans are not the only ones to have suffered, however. African Americans experienced slavery (including the great loss of life on slave ships) and forms of oppression post-emancipation; Koreans remember the trauma of Japanese occupation from 1910 to 1945; and the Chinese recall atrocities such as the rape of Nanking. My purpose is not to rehearse the particulars of these events but to emphasize that such traumatic historical events and epochs decisively shape communities and grind their theological lenses in such a way that it is impossible for them to perceive salvation merely as the path to eternity.[7] The deep wounds in the communal consciousness do not instantly heal because of the advent of more favorable circumstances, and when denial is not the order of the day, the traumatic and wounded history remains a core aspect of the communal identity. Salvation, then, is seen as a concern for the present as well as the future.

A good example of this concern is seen in the way Luke 4:18–19 might be read. When Jesus quotes Isaiah 61:1–2 and applies it to himself, what kind of Messiah is perceived by those who are oppressed or have a history of oppression? In Luke 4, Jesus addresses covenant people who are in a Canaanite-like dispossession, for they are under the rule of Rome. They are oppressed, but they are also ethnocentric. Jesus declares himself to be the Messiah, but his mission extends to all people, not just the Jews, as the subsequent references to the widow in Zarephath and Naaman show (vv. 24–27). This text shows God's concern for the larger world and his concern for well-being in this life.[8]

---

7. It is interesting to note, for example, how feudal society decisively shaped the soteriological vision of Anselm, as seen in *Cur Deus Homo?* It clearly reflected the experiences of the people in his era.

8. My thanks to Rikk Watts for his insights on this passage.

Members of oppressed communities tend to see a Messiah who has come with good news, and that news refers to their physical deliverance. It is true they may also perceive spiritual rescue, but their lenses are ground in such a way that they see a Jesus who has come to address their immediate, concrete concerns. This is a Jesus who actually cares about their plight, who brings divine justice to their cause. From their perspective, they are the poor, the captives, and the oppressed in Isaiah and Luke. Their theological vision leads these communities to inquire, "Where is God, and how will he care for our plight?"

A helpful concept for such a soteriology is the Asian concept of *han* as articulated by Korean theologians. John T. Kim defines *han* as "a deep feeling that rises out of the unjust, suppressed, amassed and condensed experience of oppression caused by mischief or misfortune so that it forms a kind of 'lump' in one's spirit."[9] Andrew Sung Park adds to this the fact that *han* can be understood collectively. The collective experience of *han* is most relevant to this discussion. He says, "Collective *han* can be interpreted two ways. One is the collective reality of individual experiences of *han*. The other is the experience of a group of people."[10]

While *han* is an Asian concept, its content is broadly applicable to other oppressed groups. Asians are not the only ones with lumps in their spirits because of past or present experiences of oppression. *Han* helps explain how African Americans, for example, can continue to speak about great injustices even when a significant segment of the group has achieved socioeconomic success. For the oppressed, the experience of *han* precipitates soteriological questions oriented toward the resolution of oppression. The "lump" in the spirit, whether in the individual or in the collective consciousness, requires a solution that exceeds the assurance that one's eternal destiny is secure. The resolution of *han* requires a Messiah who will orchestrate a form of rescue from life-threatening circumstances. When is *han* resolved? Resolution does not exclude the eschaton, but its focus

9. *Protestant Church Growth in Korea* (Belleville, Ontario: Essence Publishing, 1996), 263.
10. *The Wounded Heart of God: The Asian Concept of Han and the Christian Doctrine of Sin* (Nashville: Abingdon, 1993), 36.

is a change in circumstances for the oppressed and justice brought to bear on the oppressor.

Soul-saving individualistic salvation would lead to a reading of Luke 4 with the opposite results. Many evangelicals, particularly those who are Caucasian and middle-class, do not readily read Luke's text in this concrete fashion. They do not need to because the socioeconomic system has worked well for them and oppression is a foreign experience to them.[11] As those who enjoy the fruits of hard work in society, many white evangelicals do not have a need for salvation to have an impact on their concrete existence. Since they have that part of their lives under control, they can focus on their inner world and getting to heaven. The life experience of such evangelicals grinds their theological lenses in ways that actually render them blind to readings of Scripture that may reveal sin and salvation as anything other than an individual matter. They have the luxury of viewing salvation as a matter of the heart alone. Those who have a soteriological perspective that is focused heavenward easily read Luke in a way that spiritualizes Jesus' role as deliverer of the oppressed. If Jesus came to save souls, then this text must refer to Jesus' self-understanding as the Son of God who has come to bring a spiritual kingdom in our hearts. While this is true, is that all Jesus meant? Is it at all possible that he came as a Messiah not only to transform hearts but also to bring a social revolution? It seems that he did just that, from elevating the status of women to challenging social stratification to addressing poverty.

The revolution brought by Christ was not that expected by the majority of Israel, but in a way typical of his ministry, Christ initiated a new social order. His revolution emerged through nonconventional means (it was not violent in the sense of a wartime coup, though a sword is still to come in the end) and slowly began to turn the world upside down. Members of oppressed communities then ask, "What will he do for me and my people, and how, and when?" If Jesus did more than provide a

11. Michael O. Emerson and Christian Smith, *Divided by Faith: Evangelical Religion and the Problem of Race in America* (New York: Oxford University Press, 2000) spells out the manner in which individualism has so shaped the perspective of white evangelicals that it is difficult for them to perceive structural or systemic factors in the race problem in America. Particularly see 74–91.

bridge to heaven, then evangelicals must face the following question: If we have focused on only half of the gospel, half of the truth, then do we have the truth at all?

Concrete Soteriology

The rest of this chapter discusses four categories that help articulate a soteriology that focuses on this life. The first is the *public* nature of salvation. From the perspective of the oppressed, the work of God that delivers his people cannot be merely an internal, personal relationship with Jesus Christ that provides one with a passport to heaven. The domain of salvation must go beyond individual hearts to public manifestations. In addition to issues of actual deliverance from oppression, a helpful area of inquiry when considering the public nature of salvation concerns the meaning of the cross. If it is more than just punishment for sin, what is it? What does Jesus mean in Luke 9:23 when he states that cross-bearing is essential to discipleship? When considering salvation as a public matter, this text points to the cross as a public instrument of death that is centrally related to the path of discipleship. Recalling the discussion of *han*, Andrew Sung Park articulates a view of the cross as God's protest against the oppressor. Christ's suffering on the cross identifies with the suffering of human history and is God's way of saying, "Enough is enough" to the oppressors.[12]

Park writes, "To Jesus Christ, calling the Pharisees 'children of vipers' was a harsh challenge to them. In like manner the cross is the ultimate challenge to oppressors to make their choice between repentance and eternal death."[13] The cross issues a call for the oppressor to repent, while it is also an expression of the death of the righteous in unjust circumstances. As Peter Abelard's "moral influence" account of the atonement suggests, the cross shows us an unjust public execution while calling for reversals both individual and corporate in nature.

12. Park, *Wounded Heart of God*, 124. It is of interest to note that Park sees the cross as God's *han* erupted in the middle of history. God is considered to have *han* because of his misery and anguish with his people, as seen in the Book of Hosea, for example.
13. Ibid.

Further, it demonstrates that righteousness brings a public cost. Those who walk after Jesus and protest for righteousness must reckon with the potential of death. To follow the way of the cross is to say to the world that one is committed not only to personal holiness but also to public holiness, which may invite ruin from the hand of the powers that rule unjustly. The public aspect of salvation is not always victory in this life, even as it is legitimately pursued.

While it is a public event that displays God's resolution of personal sin, the cross may also serve as the symbol of costly discipleship. A way to think of this is to consider the relationship between following Christ and lynching. The point is not that all victims of lynching were Christians but that some victims of lynching were targets because they called for God's justice in the era of Jim Crow.[14] Given the church-driven nature of the African-American struggle for justice, we can see the antagonized communities as communities of cross-bearers who were aware that following Christ meant demanding justice, regardless of the ultimate cost.

Does salvation as a public concern mean that the Christian faith should prompt forms of community life that may invite death? While the answer may be an obvious yes, life in the West rarely presents stakes that are so high. Certainly our Korean Christian brothers and sisters who perished because they refused to bow to the image of the Emperor during the Japanese occupation knew this cost. The fellowship of martyrs knows well the cost of discipleship as public allegiance and activity.

The question for evangelical soteriology is this: How do we move forward in articulating salvation as a costly public identification with a Messiah who may bring about deliverance in this life through the suffering of a cross-bearing community? If

14. "Jim Crow" is a term used to describe the legal race-based segregation that took place in the United States after post–Civil War Reconstruction ended in 1877 until the mid-1960s. These laws, rules, and customs led to such things as segregated schools, water fountains labeled "white" and "colored," and the relegation of African Americans to the back of buses in public transportation. While such rules supposedly allowed for a "separate but equal" society, the Jim Crow laws took away the rights from African Americans gained through the Thirteenth, Fourteenth, and Fifteenth Amendments. Jim Crow laws legitimized treating African Americans as second-class citizens or less.

agitating for justice is part of the public character of salvation, how do we express this costly discipleship in a manner that evangelical ears will hear?

One statement to this effect is that Christians who claim to have given their hearts to Jesus while failing to call for justice, particularly those in positions of influence, may unwittingly have joined themselves to the enemy in their life practice. Though they may give to missions, attend church regularly, and engage in daily personal devotions, their lives, apart from inner piety, are no different from those of the unsaved. Will evangelical piety break free from the inner life and have a public impact, thereby changing the circumstances of Christian brothers and sisters who suffer? If not, are we really who we say we are?

Second, salvation focused on this life is *political* in character. Political theologies abound, many focused on liberation and many explicitly anti-Western and anti-capitalistic. Salvation does not have to be politically left- or right-wing for one to acknowledge that salvation addresses social and structural change as well as transformed hearts. As Michael Emerson and Christian Smith show,[15] this is not an easy move to make for white evangelicals in the United States, but difficulty does not mean inevitable intractability on the matter. Recognition of the social and structural character of sin and salvation can become a significant part of evangelical soteriology—as seen in the work of Ronald Sider, for example.[16]

A belief that salvation contains social and structural aspects leads to a discussion of corporate sin. Sin is not often articulated in this manner in evangelical theology texts, though there are exceptions (such as Millard Erickson's). Yet the Bible, particularly in the Old Testament, reveals sin as both individual and corporate. Consider the following examples: Achan's sin in Joshua 7 leads to corporate disaster in battle; Nehemiah's prayer (Neh. 1:6–7) confesses the sin of the people as a whole, not the aggregate sins of individuals; 2 Chronicles 7:14, a favorite evangelical text, urges the people of God to turn to him in repentance, saying he will respond by forgiving and blessing the

15. See Emerson and Smith, *Divided by Faith*, 51–133.
16. See his *Good News and Good Works: A Theology for the Whole Gospel* (Grand Rapids: Baker, 1999).

nation; Daniel prays for his city and people in Daniel 9; Micah 3 indicts the leaders of Israel for oppressing the people. These texts demonstrate that sin can be considered corporately and structurally. Sin perpetuates itself in the lives of individuals and in the systems constructed to oppress, marginalize, and exterminate "others." The solution to this sin comes by means of the political nature of salvation. The social structures themselves must be overturned and banished, just as the moneychangers were cast out when Jesus cleansed the temple. While the moneychangers may have set up shop again the next day, the cue for Christians is to put them out of business or to change their practices.

If Christians perpetuate systems that practice blatant and subtle forms of oppression, how might God respond? Israel was taken into exile not only because of idolatry but also because of systemic injustice. In the West, many delight to call themselves the covenant people of God, but are these people also ready for the responsibility that comes with such a role? Are they ready to accept negative consequences for perpetuating corporate sin? Or to put the question differently, are they ready to bring justice, even if changes to the socioeconomic system come at a cost to them?

Evangelicals can ill afford either to ignore corporate sin or to recognize it only when it comes to roost in their comfort zone. If we are really people of the Book, we must read all of it and get beyond what is often a strictly Pauline soteriology that articulates sin as an individual matter resolved by forensic justification. This requires a change in thinking that, if Emerson and Smith are correct, cannot come about if white evangelicals remain cocooned in a comfortable ghetto. Extended interaction with Christians who have a deep understanding of social and structural sin is necessary.

In spite of this necessity, the difficulty often inherent in such interaction frequently leaves many participants frustrated. How do we reach a place where such interaction is typical rather than exceptional? We need considerable wisdom, which we can get only from God but which is accessible to us as his covenant people indwelt by the Holy Spirit. Much has quenched the Spirit in regard to the political aspect of salvation, but a checkered history should not prevent us from taking what will be a difficult path. It is my prayer that I do not walk the path alone.

Third, salvation focused on this life is *pneumatological*. The doctrine of the Holy Spirit, while generally neglected, is often related to spiritual life in non-tangible sometimes mystical ways when it is the focus of reflection. It is indeed true that the Spirit reunites us to God and orients us toward heaven, but if we limit pneumatology to regeneration and the exercise of spiritual gifts, we reflect a truncated perspective. As Arnold A. Van Ruler has argued, the work of the Spirit leads us to focus "on us and our world. The goal is that we ourselves become images of God and experience this world as his kingdom. This is what the Spirit does to us. The Spirit is poured out and dwells with and in us. . . . We have a zest for the world."[17] Van Ruler asserts that the Spirit indwells not only Christians but also nations and cultures as they are taken up into the covenant. While one may challenge this latter view as triumphalist, Van Ruler does push us in a helpful direction by calling our attention to the Spirit's work in orienting us toward life in the here and now, not just toward an eternal future.

For those who are oppressed, the stress of this life requires divine action to resolve injustice. If evangelicals believe that salvation involves a zeal for the world, they will cast their gaze toward the concrete particulars of this life and pursue the resolution of injustice. A question that must be addressed concerns eschatology. Does a pneumatological orientation toward this life demand a postmillennial eschatology or the pursuit of a theocracy? Must one be postmillennial in orientation to believe that structural sin can be redeemed in this life? The answer is no, though I acknowledge that pretribulational-premillennial eschatology (still a dominant perspective) may not resonate well with this approach. As long as proponents of this view keep their gaze heavenward, attention given to the concrete particulars of this life rather than to the great escape will be an exception. Amillennial and historic premillennial perspectives can allow for the resolution of structural sin in the present, partic-

17. *Calvinist Trinitarianism and Theocentric Politics: Essays toward a Public Theology*, trans. John Bolt (Lewiston, N.Y.: Edward Mellen, 1989), 39.

ularly since they emphasize the partial presence of the kingdom, even if some proponents of these views consider social transformation to be imperfect. Even a partial realization of the kingdom in society, though imperfect, is preferable to leaving the oppressed to wait for the consummation of the age. If we agree that the Spirit directs our gaze to this life and that Jesus brings justice in even a partial sense today, then we ought to consider the pursuit of societal transformation as essential to our sanctification as personal holiness. We should be concerned if our salvation does not lead to actions that reveal our love for our brothers and sisters who remain oppressed. A Spirit-led revolution still beckons.

The final point, and perhaps the most literally concrete, is that salvation focused on this life emphasizes the need for a *place*. Oppression is often attended by the dispossession of land, the literal displacement of a group of people. As noted above, many oppressed groups were taken from or driven from their homes, many times by Christians who advocated slavery or colonization. In the consciousness of some oppressed people, there is a longing for a return to a place that can be called home. Growing up as an African American, I have become familiar with the discourse in some circles that calls for a return to Africa or, more simply, for a true life as a citizen of the United States. Concrete soteriology recognizes that we were created to be at home somewhere and does not gloss over that fact by trumpeting the slogan, "I'm just passing through this world." While here, this life is not to be merely survived, particularly in nations and communities in which other Christians flourish. The prayer for a true home is not sub-Christian as long as it is not a source of idolatry. The cry of the oppressed for salvation in this life includes a desire for a safe place to dwell.[18]

A concrete soteriology, however, does not necessarily call for restitution in which the oppressors are sent away and the land returned to the dispossessed. Rather, reconciliation is the goal, particularly in social contexts in which Christians are spread

18. Someone may say, "What about missionaries? They are never really at home anywhere." This is true, but it is also the case that missionaries are sent to their various destinations, not displaced or made to feel that they do not belong in a community or society in which they wish to dwell in peace.

across the social strata. Revelation 7:9 presents a picture of a diversified populace around the throne, and soteriology focused on this life is oriented toward prefiguring that great scene. The goal then becomes a truly integrated society without blanket cultural assimilation, a rich and kaleidoscopic community that has made it possible for the formerly oppressed to flourish in this life. Rather than telling our less fortunate brothers and sisters to hold on until they get to heaven, we need to tell them, "You, too, have a place that you can call home." Having said that, it is important to keep the concrete sense of place in tension with the pilgrimage aspect of our faith. The best earthly circumstances will never match the new heavens and earth. Yet this reality does not mean that asceticism should be forced on the less fortunate. While we are here, we need to seek the best for all those around us. This means that they should have a true sense of place.

Conclusion

So what is *this life* for? Seeing salvation as public, political, pneumatological, and providing a sense of place leads us to take our sojourn on earth with great seriousness. Rather than simply longing for heaven, we long for a world that will see God's justice roll down in the transformation of social structures and systems that preserve injustice and oppress various people groups. Recognizing that our oppressed brothers and sisters cry out for a resolution to their *han*, we direct our zeal for the world toward their cause. We do not do this by hopping on to every cause that presents itself without discernment. But at the same time, we have no excuse for ignoring injustice and chalking it up to a world that is in a helpless descent into chaos before the rapture. It is important that as evangelicals we ask ourselves the following question: If we claim to have experienced God's liberation and rest, can we be sure we have not deceived ourselves by failing to participate in the justice that Jesus brings? Salvation is not merely a heavenly hope. It provides confidence that this life is meaningful, regardless of circumstance, and the anticipation that we can experience a world that sees God's grace revealed in concrete, transformative ways.

5

Being Saved as a New Creation

Co-Humanity in the True Imago Dei

CHERITH FEE NORDLING

A Necessary Question

In the wake of September 11, 2001, the question "What does it mean to be saved?" seems a crucial one to be asking as we see human beings violently devaluing the lives of other human beings, truly believing them to be subhuman on the basis of race, religion, sex, privilege, or some other cultural or social determination. Having thus diminished or even dismissed the other's human dignity and worth, the way is paved for those who deem themselves superior to marginalize, ostracize, subordinate, even annihilate the less-than-human other.

The question becomes a necessary one in such a broken world because it is not only a soteriological one, having to do with how and why we are saved, but also a thoroughly ontological one. That is, it asks what it means to *be*—in this case, to *be human* in the image of God. To restate the original question along these lines, we ask, "What does it mean for us as women and men to be saved from our sinful and broken humanity, to have our *imago Dei* redeemed and restored as a new creation in and through Jesus Christ, and to live in relational and ethical correspondence to that present and future reality?" What does it mean to have our *human being* transformed and grounded in the true image of God, corporately and individually shaped by his Spirit? In this sense, to ask, "What does it mean to be saved?" is to ask about *being human, being in Christ,* and *being in the Spirit* as differentiated but ontologically equal participants in Christ's body.

Before we begin to answer this question, however, let us first clarify what we are *not* asking by noting two common but different questions that often reflect remnants of the broken image rather than the restored *imago Dei* given in the true human, Jesus Christ.

Excursus: Two Alternate Questions

How Do I Get Saved?

First, we are *not* asking the ever familiar evangelical question "What does it mean to *get* saved?" Our question is one of human *being,* not private human attainment. Too often we describe *being* saved as "getting" or "having" Jesus Christ as our "personal" Lord and Savior. Here the amazing grace of the truly "personal" encounter between God and humanity tends to have less to do with God's Triune Personhood and covenanting love for and among his creation than with our personalized religious experience. Furthermore, in a culture of personal acquisition and pluralistic accommodation, "getting saved" can quickly turn Jesus into a commodity on the shelf of religious options. Western individualism and consumerism meet religious marketing: "Yes, you too can have your very own personal Savior to meet your every need," or worse, "Try Jesus—you'll like him, and you'd be doing him such a favor." This tendency and its second-order manifestation of church "shopping" based on personal preference are rife among evangelicals and are sadly apparent even to those outside the church. As nonbeliever Tom Waits sings, "Don't go to church on Sunday / Don't get me on my knees to pray / Don't memorize the books of the Bible / I got my own special way. / Well it's got to be a chocolate Jesus / Make me feel good inside / Got to be a chocolate Jesus / Keep me satisfied."[1]

Then again, it might be that our theological orientation requires us to reverse the metaphor. God is shopping; he's written out his list in advance, checked it twice, and we sure hope we're on it. Or, shifting metaphors altogether, we hope to win the predestination lottery or do whatever is necessary to activate our eternal life insurance policy. These exaggerations simply serve to show that even when "getting saved" revolves around the idea of God's electing action rather than ours, we often reduce this mystery to a matter of individual, eternal security—"getting it right" to get into heaven. The *imago Dei*, the relational, corporate union and communion of men and women together for and with one another and God is replaced by the narcissistic, individual self who functions as the central subject in every narrative—even the biblical one. Suddenly, God exists for the creature rather than the creature for God and his creation, particularly other human beings. Somehow *we* "have" God rather than God "having" us. We are blinded to the revelation that we have been created for God's eternal pleasure and communion but that God, through his own Being-Act in Christ and the Spirit, has done everything necessary to make such communion possible.

This is not to dismiss, however, the individual, unique encounter between God and each of his children. The marvel of the Christian faith and the heart of the gospel is that God seeks, restores, and saves his broken children *one at a time*. The shepherd really leaves the ninety-nine to search for the one lost sheep. The woman does not stop searching for her lost coin to be content with the remainder. The father who thought his son was lost does race down the road to crush his child into his arms, lavishly celebrating his homecoming and being outdone by the heavenly hosts. God finds us in our sin, one by one, and brings us home.

But that's just it. He doesn't then set up individual, relational dyads with us. He doesn't go off and have a "one-on-one" with the lost sheep. The sheep is rejoined with the flock, where it finds its

1. Tom Waits, "Chocolate Jesus," *Mule Variations* (1999).

life, safety, and identity under the care of the shepherd *with* the other sheep. The coin is put back with the rest of what perhaps is the woman's dowry. The "disgraced" son is restored with honor and love to his position in the household, much to his "faithful" brother's chagrin. Our heavenly Father brings us home, gives us new birth by his Spirit, and in Jesus restores us to the relational reality that defines us (John 3:1–8; Romans 8). He brings us back into relationship, first with the divine communion of Father, Son, and Holy Spirit and then into the human community formed ontologically *by* and *in* that divine communion.

The idea of a dyadic, privatized relationship with God—particularly as an expression of salvation—is theologically impossible for Christians. Because God in his own being is one God in three Persons, there is no possibility of relating to God as the divine, solitary Other. Relationship with God is always and forever participation in the preexisting *koinōnia* of the divine Persons. This is why the two essential sacraments in the life of the "saved ones" in the new creation—baptism (a celebration of our *individual* death and new life in Christ by the Spirit) and the communion meal (an ongoing celebration of the gracious ontological reality of our *corporate* life together with God and one another)—are always consecrated in the Triune name. It is this God who has created us and given us our relational being and identity in his image.

In sum, if we ask about "getting saved" in terms of human acquisition or a privatized divine-human relationship, we are asking from a distorted understanding of the true *imago Dei*.

What Is Salvation?

Neither is our question about salvation posed in an abstract or metaphorical sense. As evangelicals our answers would undoubtedly center around an understanding of salvation as deliverance from sin through the life, death, and resurrection of Christ and new life in the kingdom of God. Nevertheless, we tend to get bogged down in systematic distinctions between atonement, justification, conversion, sanctification, grace, law, and divine and human freedom. Unfortunately, by arguing over technicalities, we often lose the realization that God's salvific Being-Act of creation, redemption, and consummation is, at the end of the day, still the *mystery* of God's being *for us*.[2]

Alternatively, when the question of salvation is raised as a human possibility, as in liberal, liberation, or constructivist contexts, it is often in abstraction from the historical reality of Jesus Christ crucified, risen, and exalted. In these contexts, the miraculous particularity of his life ceases to be both God's self-revelation and, simultaneously, the revelation of our own broken *imago Dei*—that God's free self-determination in love and mercy to be for us in Jesus Christ was also his choice of necessary judgment on himself for our sin. Failure to recognize this dual reality creates problems of an entirely different sort.

When salvation is considered apart from the Triune God's incarnate presence among us, then the understanding of human beings as *imago Dei* ceases to acknowledge that God, whom we image, both precedes us and has made his own name and identity known to us in human history. This abstraction opens the way for a prioritizing of human being, existence, and knowledge as determinate of who or what God is and with it the human determination of what constitutes divine freedom. The classic, narcissistic inversion of sin occurs, what Luther called the *incurvatus in se* of fallen humanity. Turning in on ourselves, the *imago* suddenly precedes the *Dei*, and God is consciously fashioned after our own image, be it Asian, white, male, black, female, patriarchal king, earth goddess, Ground of Being, or what have you.

As the saying goes, God made us in his image (Gen. 1:26–27; 5:1), and we have forever been trying to return the compliment. We continue to reenact the original idolatry that defines human sinfulness by assuming not only that we can know God apart from his own self-revelation but also that we creatures know better—and thus more—than our Creator. We can both save ourselves and name "God" from our own self-created identity, blurring the necessary distinction between the divine and the human in the process. Ultimately, God ceases to be the personal Other who reveals his own Triune being as Father, Son,

2. While "salvation in Christ" is arguably the theme of Paul's entire theology, our question does not allow us to dissect each aspect of that larger reality or to attempt to describe its totality in Christian doctrine.

and Spirit and is instead viewed as an empty tabula rasa on which to draw human self-portraits.

From this perspective, sin is minimalized or negated altogether.[3] Rather than being an insurmountable, death-producing human condition apart from the grace of God in Christ, "sin" describes specific or systemic forms of injustice that humans can both abolish and replace with justice and love through their own will and action. The atoning death of Christ on the cross is a thoroughly unnecessary idea and even an offensive one, an expression of cosmic child abuse befitting the patriarchal God of classical theology long since rejected by contemporary thought.[4] As Rosemary Radford Ruether summarizes:

> [We] reject the classical notion that the human soul is radically fallen, alienated from God, and unable to make any move to reconcile itself to God, therefore needing an outside mediator. . . . Instead the human self is defined through its primary identity as image of God. This original goodness and communion with its divine "ground of being" *continue to be* "our *true nature.*" [The seriousness of evil and its human element do] . . . not change our potential for good. We are alienated or out of touch with this potential, but experiences of consciousness-raising . . . begin a process of conversion, *getting back in touch with a better self* and reconstructing personal and social relations. An external redeemer is not necessary for this process of conversion, since we have not lost our true self rooted in God.[5]

Salvation, as getting in touch with one's better self and then reconstructing the world accordingly, is ultimately an ideal

3. In our highly "therapized" mainline and evangelical traditions as well, sin is an increasingly "unpopular" concept. For an excellent discussion of this in regard to the narcissistic self, see Alan J. Torrance, "The Self-Relation, Narcissism, and the Gospel of Grace," *Scottish Journal of Theology* 40 (1987): 481–510.

4. Jesus the human was certainly not "God come to die" in what Catholic feminist Elizabeth Johnson describes as a masochistic desire for victim status. Instead, Jesus' death was "an act of violence brought about by threatened human men, as sin, and therefore *against the will* of a gracious God." See Elizabeth A. Johnson, "Jesus and Salvation," The Catholic Theological Society of America, *Proceedings* 49 (1994): 15; and idem, *She Who Is: The Mystery of God in Feminist Theological Discourse* (New York: Crossroads, 1992), 158.

5. Rosemary Radford Ruether, *Women and Redemption* (New York: Fortress, 1998), 275, emphasis added.

shaped by a particular self-image or worldview used to promote the agenda of a particular people or cause. Garrett
Green describes this as "role play" theology, a repristination
of what Ludwig Feuerbach and Karl Barth critiqued as the essence of natural theology, namely, God-talk as human self-
projection.[6] Ruether and her colleagues work from the assumption that the unknowable God is known through our
"full humanness" as untainted "image of God." From this perspective, "all of our images of God are human projections. God
in Godself is beyond human words and images, only partly
and metaphorically expressed in any images. The question is:
What are worse projections that promote injustice and diminished humanness, and what are better projections that promote fuller humanness?"[7]

The Christian tradition, however, assumes not only that
we are hopelessly bound by sin and thus unable either to
save ourselves or restore the broken *imago Dei,* hence recon-
ciling our relationships with God and one another, but also
that we are not able even to *perceive* the gift of God in Christ
that will save and restore us without God's revealing, empowering Spirit. We are utterly dependent on the self-giving
gift of God in Jesus Christ to redeem and restore creation to
its ultimate glory, specifically to renew us as men and women
to full personhood in divine and human communion, putting to death what is broken and living the life of the new
creation *in Christ* by the Spirit. It is only in the human-di-
vine being of Jesus Christ, the true *imago Dei* who lived his
human life in obedience to the Father by the power of the
Spirit, that we live and move and have *our human being*
(Acts 17:24–31).

To ask about salvation apart from Jesus Christ, the image of
the invisible God and the firstborn over all creation (Col. 1:15),

6. Garrett Green, "The Gender of God and the Theology of Metaphor," in
Speaking the Christian God: The Holy Trinity and the Challenge of Feminism, ed.
Alvin F. Kimel, Jr. (Grand Rapids: Eerdmans, 1992), 44–64.
7. Rosemary Radford Ruether, "Christian Tradition and Feminist Hermeneutics," in *The Image of God: Gender Models in Judeo-Christian Tradition,* ed.
Kari Børresen (Minneapolis: Fortress, 1995), 286. This approach is endorsed
by such constructivist, process, and liberation-revisionist theologians as Gordon Kaufman, Sallie McFague, Anna Case-Winters, and Elizabeth Johnson.

the true Adam (Rom. 5:12–21), is again to ask from a distorted sense of the true *imago Dei*—in this case, from a distorted view of human beings as sinless images, even imagers, of God.

This brings us back to the question of what it means to *be* saved. I contend that to be saved is to be renewed in the true image of God as women and men in Christ, to have our relationality restored so that our sinful selves, hopelessly *incurvatus in se*, are set free to *be* new creations in true divine and human *koinōnia*. To that end we now turn.

Being a New Creation in Christ, the True Image of God and Humanity

Colin Gunton emphasizes that creation has a future direction and directedness toward perfection and completeness. Creation is not merely *through* Christ but *to* him in its eschatological thrust toward completion *in* him. Hence, salvation history is not a series of divine interventions but a story of unerring divine love and purpose, achieving the original purpose of creation.[8]

> For he chose us in him *before the creation of the world* to be holy and blameless in his sight. In love he predestined us to be adopted as his sons through Jesus Christ, in accordance with his pleasure and will. . . . He made known to us *the mystery of his will* according to his good pleasure, which he purposed in Christ, to be put into effect when the times will have reached their fulfillment—*to bring all things in heaven and on earth together under one head, even Christ.*
>
> Ephesians 1:4–5, 9–10, emphasis added

In this sense, Scripture does not describe salvation as "creation—plan B" or the new covenant as a rescue operation. Being saved, being in covenantal relation, is God's first and only eternal plan of creation. He spoke it into being by his Word, gave it life by his Spirit, and brought about its historical realization in Christ as the fulfillment of "the mystery of his will" and his "plan for the fullness of time, to unite all things in

8. Colin Gunton, *Christ and Creation* (Grand Rapids: Eerdmans, 1990), 95–97.

him, things in heaven and on earth" (Col. 1:19–20). In the mystery of his will, God intended to be both Lord of creation and *part* of it. The Word, who in the beginning was *with* God, who *was* God, and who made all things, became flesh and dwelt among us, and in him we beheld the glory of God (John 1:1–2, 14). In this way, God became one with broken humanity to restore it to its true divine likeness.

Though the New Testament draws allusions to Old Testament passages that refer to humanity in "the image of God"[9] (notably in 1 Cor. 11:7 and James 3:9),[10] the apostle Paul uniquely reserves the term, at least in the first instance, for Jesus Christ (e.g., 2 Cor. 4:4). Paul describes Jesus as "the image of the invisible God" *and* "the firstborn over all creation" (Col. 1:15). This theme is taken up by the author of Hebrews when he writes, "The Son is the radiance of God's glory and the exact representation *[charaktēr]* of his being" and *also* the fully human, flesh-and-blood image who suffered and tasted death *with* and *for* everyone (Heb. 1:3; 2:9). These passages hold together the revelation of Jesus Christ as the divine Son who both images and manifests the glory of the Father

9. The Old Testament gives little explicit attention to the notion of humanity in the image of God apart from the well-known texts in Genesis (1:26–27; 5:1–2). Dr. Watts's essay, however, provides grounds for an *implicit* understanding within Hebraic culture and Scripture. Two apocryphal references also offer rich interpretations of the *imago Dei*. See Sir. 17:1–13 and Wis. 2:23.

10. While the passage in 1 Corinthians that makes reference to man as the image *(eikōn)* and glory *(doxa)* of God and to woman as the glory *(doxa)* of man is difficult to reconcile with the implications of Genesis 5:1–2, which describes men and women in the likeness of God to be humanly constituted as differentiated yet complementary *ʾādām*, commentators agree that Paul is not offering a commentary on the *imago Dei* at this point. Rather, concerned with safeguarding the dignity and distinction of women in the corporate worship gathering amid the eschatological tensions in the Corinthian context, Paul is more interested in the term "glory" immediately following "image," which he develops in relation to women. See, e.g., Gordon Fee, *The First Epistle to the Corinthians* (Grand Rapids: Eerdmans, 1987), 514–15ff.; and C. K. Barrett, *First Epistle to the Corinthians* (London: Adam & Charles Black, 1968), 288–89. The passage in James parallels the ethical concerns in Genesis 9:6, but it is cursing with the tongue that is prohibited based on humanity in the *imago Dei*. I am grateful to Murray Rae's unpublished lecture, King's College, November 1998, for this reference and for his work on the *imago Dei*.

and images the true form of created humanity. He is both humanity's redeemer and prototype.[11]

The description of Jesus as the new Adam (Rom. 5:12–21) is in the context of God's eradication of sin as the redemptive plan for all of creation, including the restoration of the *imago Dei* in the original *ʾādām*—humankind, male and female (Gen. 5:1–2). In other words, to be restored by the new Adam, Jesus Christ, means to be brought back in to right relationship not only with God but also with other male and female human beings as fellow *ʾādām*. It is to be a new *human* creation. The implications for us are that "just as we have borne the likeness of the earthly man, so shall we bear the likeness of the man from heaven" (1 Cor. 15:49; cf. 2 Cor. 3:18). Just what, then, does this look like?

The Sacrificial, Cruciform *Imago*—To *Be* for the Other

As and from God, Jesus does not exist first for himself, nor for a cause or an idea, but for others—for God and for his fellow human beings. To *be* for others constitutes his identity as a human *being* and has its basis in his relation to God. What Jesus does for others is not done in his own name or authority. It is done in the name and loving character of the Father. This character, by its very nature, looks outward to serve the interests of the other. Jesus' existence is wholly determined by the One who sent him, as ours is wholly determined by the One who created and re-creates us, the One who chose from all eternity to be *God for us*.

The radical extent of Jesus' life for others is anticipated in his baptism and reaches its culmination in his death. He allows his own existence to be framed by his fellow human beings in their alienation, suffering, and peril. In his own person, he bears the

11. As Paul so aptly commandeers the language of the ancients, "In him we live and move and have our being. . . . We are his offspring" (Acts 17:28). Christ is the pioneer and perfector of our faith, having been made perfect (Heb. 5:9; 12:2); the righteous one or model of righteousness (Luke 23:47; 1 John 2:1; 3:7); the full stature of whom we are directed toward (Eph. 4:13); and the second Adam, the righteous one who obeys God and overcomes human alienation (Rom. 5:12–21). Our true humanity is revealed, established, safeguarded, and given as a gift to us in Christ, and only in this way can we speak of Jesus as the prototype whom we follow. We cannot attain our new, full humanity by ourselves in our brokenness.

burden of humanity's unfaithfulness, being made sin and given up for us (Rom. 8:32; 2 Cor. 5:21). This is the significance of Jesus' baptism of repentance: not that he sinned but that he bore our human nature in order to bear the cost of its restoration as our deliverer. Jesus Christ identifies himself with the first Adam in order to become the second, reconciled, and renewed Adam. In this act, which becomes the definition of his whole life, he is most truly himself—"an I who gives himself wholly to the cause and being of others."[12]

And yet, Jesus' obedience was a truly human choice enabled by the Spirit. The Spirit enabled Jesus to be the first truly human person, fulfilling the divine life of the Son by making the Father known and uniting the world to him.[13] It is no surprise that following Jesus' baptism the Spirit's first act was to lead him into the desert to face his call to human obedience unto death and in so doing to resist the evil one. Only then did he return home, assigning Isaiah's messianic word to himself— "The Spirit of the Lord is on me" (Luke 4:18; cf. Isa. 61:1)—and begin to live his life in correspondence to and fulfillment of that word (Matt. 4:23), knowing full well the suffering it would entail (Isaiah 53). In Jesus' human life, obedient to the Father and the Spirit, the great re-creative process began, reversing the effects of sin so that the blind could see and the lame could walk. The disenfranchised were included and honored, the lost were found and reconciled, the brokenhearted were comforted, and the dead were raised to life.

These two dimensions of human being—for God and for others—are to be understood, then, in terms of the empowering Spirit. As the new creation, we too are to live lives of Spirit-led

12. Rae, unpublished lecture, King's College, November 1998. Tom Wright also states, "Sacrifice is part of what it means to be truly human. . . . The sacrifice of Jesus is the moment when the human race, in the person of a single man, offers itself fully to the Creator. . . .The result is that now at last true human life is possible" (*Following Jesus* [Grand Rapids: Eerdmans, 1994], 9).

13. Throughout Scripture, and particularly in the life of Jesus, we come to see the Spirit as the Lord, the giver of life. The creating, life-giving Spirit is in the beginning hovering over the waters, breathing life into male and female as the image of God, and here again we see the creative presence of the Spirit birthing new life, making a new man in the image of God. So too the Spirit is our essential life-giver as the new creation given by Jesus Christ, the baptizer in the Holy Spirit (Matt. 3:11).

obedience, and the shape of this new life together is, very simply, cruciform. Crucified with Christ, we also live with Christ.
What is the norm for that life? To be for the other, to "carry
each other's burdens" and so "fulfill the law of Christ," which is
to say, the pattern of Christ's own selfless life of obedience manifest in love for the other (Gal. 6:2). Losing his life by living for
others, Jesus broke all the patterns of conformity of his day,
and this nonconformity is required of those who are conformed
to his image: "If anyone would come after me, he must deny
himself and take up his cross and follow me. For whoever wants
to save his life will lose it, and whoever loses his life for me will
find it" (Matt. 16:24–25).

The only way to live the cruciform life for others is by constantly relying on, walking in, keeping in step with, and living
in the Spirit (Gal. 2:20; 5:25), who conforms and transforms us
in Christ (Rom. 8:29; 12:2). This radically dependent life is,
ironically, the ultimately free life. No longer bound to this fallen
world as slaves to its cultural expectations, we are free to be servants of the one who took on himself "the nature of a slave"
(Phil. 2:7). As female and male, rich and poor, Asian and black,
Catholic and Baptist children, we are Abraham's true seed and
heirs of the promise who have been set free to *be* for and with
one another, no longer treating one another as commodities to
be exploited or as competitors to be defeated but as fellow
human beings, equal recipients of God's saving grace and new
life.

Life Together as Women and Men in Radical Conformity to Christ

To be saved, then, to be *in Christ,* is to submit to a complete
overhaul of our relational life that we may form one people of
God. Paul is unrelenting in this regard. Every epistle to the
churches reminds them of their call to walk as a people who derive their new life from the being of Jesus Christ. For instance,
to the Colossians he says:

> Do not lie to each other, since you have taken off your old self
> with its practices and have put on the new self, which is being
> renewed in knowledge *in the image of its Creator.* Here there is

no Greek or Jew, circumcised or uncircumcised, barbarian, Scythian, slave or free, but Christ is all, and is in all.

3:9–11, emphasis added

And again, to the Galatians, who, having begun life by the Spirit, were forgetting who(se) they were:

You are all sons of God through faith in Christ Jesus, for all of you who were baptized into Christ have clothed yourselves with Christ. There is neither Jew nor Greek, neither slave nor free, male nor female, for you are all one in Christ Jesus. If you be- long to Christ, then you are Abraham's seed, and heirs according to the promise.

3:26–29

Paul asserts in these passages that when people come into the fellowship of Jesus Christ so that their humanity is identi- fied with his perfect image, their human dignity, value, and sta- tus are no longer based on these distinctions and their cultural connotations but on the equalizing realities of grace, the ser- vant-nature of the Lord Jesus Christ, and the gift-giving Spirit. The significance of this affirmation lies in that it equally *disad- vantages* all by equally *advantaging* all, because in Christ these distinctions do not define human personhood or position.[14] Such distinctions had no relational or social meaning to Jesus, whose values and behavior modeled the great leveling of re- deemed humanity in the kingdom, where the vineyard owner extends his grace equally and "unfairly" to everyone no matter how long they work, thus making the last first and the first last. In other words, the old creation stands under the judgment of God and is passing away (1 Cor. 7:31). Thus, we as a new cre- ation fundamentally do not belong to the age in which we re- side (Rom. 12:1–2). Our identity, values, and practices come from the future, which is already present.

However, while the distinctions of the former age cease to give value to persons, personal distinctions are not eradicated in the age of the Spirit. Just the opposite. When Paul says that these distinctions are no more, he is not eliminating difference. On the contrary, uniqueness is to be cherished. His repeated

14. Gordon D. Fee, "Galatians 3:28 and the New Creation," (unpublished).

imagery of the body and its multiple parts could hardly be more explicit regarding the diversity of our unity in the Spirit that stems from God's own Triune Being. Paul elaborates the theme of body life versus human distinctions and divisions:

> For we were all baptized by one Spirit into one body—whether Jews or Greeks, slave or free. . . . Now the body is not made up of one part but of many. . . . God has combined the members of the body and has given greater honor to the parts that lacked it, so that there should be no division in the body, but that its parts should have equal concern for each other. If one part suffers, every part suffers with it; if one part is honored, every part rejoices with it.
>
> 1 Corinthians 12:13–14, 24–26

What Paul argues *against* is giving priority to certain parts of the body or assigning privilege to certain distinctions over others, thus rebuilding the dividing wall of hostility that Christ has broken down. In Christ, people are free to be Jews, Greeks, males, females, slaves, or free and have these distinctions matter in terms of their distinctiveness and yet not matter in terms of their relational lives lived for the other.[15] To live in and under the sphere of the old realm of the flesh instead of in the new realm of the Spirit (Romans 8; Galatians 5), is to live, as Michael Gorman puts it, a "reverse anachronism." It is to allow the old to live, out of place, within the new.[16]

15. This is also reflected in the passage in Luke 20. Jesus is describing relations between men and women in the context of marriage based on the values and legislation of the old age versus the eschatological reorientation of the age to come. In Luke's Gospel, those considered worthy of a place in the resurrection have adopted the values and behaviors characteristic of the coming age. Their human worth is granted by God rather than through men's self-justification and promotion for position and prestige (Luke 10:29; 16:15; 18:9) or, in the case of women, their contractual value based on family name, heritage, and the ability to procreate. The character of the children of the resurrection, says Jesus, is marked by love of enemies, giving without expectation, and showing mercy and forgiveness (6:35–36) in the great re-creation. Joel B. Green, *The Gospel of Luke* (Grand Rapids: Eerdmans, 1997), 720–21.

16. *Cruciformity: Paul's Narrative Spirituality of the Cross* (Grand Rapids: Eerdmans, 2001), 354. See also Linda Woodhead, "God, Gender, and Identity," 12–13 (available from author).

Paul's challenge to this new people of God, God's new creation, is that if they are to take Jesus' human life and lordship seriously, they must live in correspondence to his radical reorientation of human relations in the kingdom of God. Jesus, the perfect and perfected human, demonstrated relationships that were characteristic of his Father, the God of the fatherless and the widow, the alien and the disenfranchised, the poor and the oppressed—in short, those in need of a Savior. As Jesus ushered in the new covenant, he demonstrated the extent to which God's compassion continues to go beyond any social conventions or relational norms established by broken humanity. He addressed women as equals, gave honor and recognition to children, and championed the poor and outcast. He mingled with human beings of different class, race, status, and gender, eating and communing with them and thus equalizing his and their mutual relation under God.

In particular, Jesus boldly challenged the patriarchal and prejudicial structures that upheld society by gathering followers who included women as well as men. In fact, the relatively few stories that make up the Gospel narratives are weighted heavily toward Jesus' encounters with women, and they are not incidental but essential to the plot. The narratives describe these women as firsthand witnesses to the kingdom of God through the person and work of Jesus in their own lives. These encounters range from unconventional social interactions and a stoning intervention to angelic visitations, healings, acts of deliverance, words of knowledge and forgiveness—even the initial resurrection appearances. These women were included among those upon whom the Spirit was poured out equally at Pentecost as promised by the prophet Joel (2:28–29). In other words, these non-persons with no human dignity in their culture were made human persons in relationship with God and man in a way that was essential to the telling of God's re-creative story and to an understanding of new humanity.

Why does this matter? It matters because a woman's person and station were the most undesirable of any in that day. According to Diogenes Laertius, Socrates used to say that there were three blessings for which he was grateful to Fortune: "first, that I was born a human being, and not one of the brutes; next that I was born a man and not a woman; thirdly, a Greek and not a barbarian."[17] The Jewish version, as influenced by Greco-Roman culture, told of a rabbi who said, "Every day you should say, 'Blessed are you, O God, . . . that I'm not a brute creature, nor a Gentile, nor a woman.'"[18]

While we may think that such attitudes do not prevail in Christian theology, the fact is that they have manifested themselves in both official church teaching and practice over the centuries, from Augustine and Aquinas to certain prominent evangelicals today. This is not simply a conception of women's functional subordination but of their ontological subordination.[19] By virtue of their sexual distinction, women were viewed as an inferior form of humanity.[20] In this context, Catholic feminists are asking, "If only what is assumed is redeemed and yet some ontologically superior difference attains to 'male' humanity, then has women's humanity been taken up in Christ's humanity or not?" One must ask how far this really is from, "Blessed are you, O God, that I'm not a woman"? Thus, Loren Wilkinson has aptly stated, "The deepest feminist cry has always been not, 'I want to have power' but, 'I want to be human.'"[21] An understanding of women and men as being in Christ by the Spirit continues to lag behind, though it originally

17. *Vit. Phil.*, 1.33, Loeb Classical Library.

18. Talmudic tractate *Menahoth* 43b (Epstein translation).

19. This is identical to the kind of subordination imposed on the basis of race in the early covenantal theology of colonial South Africa or the United States, where both Africans and women were subhumans or non-persons. It is the same ontological subordination applied to Jews by the "Christian" *Kulturprotestantismus* of Nazi Germany or attributed to all "Westerners" by certain Muslim fanatics typified in the actions of September 11, 2001.

20. The Thomistic theology, in opposition to which Catholic feminism arose, reflects Aquinas's medieval reception of Aristotelian biology, according to which the male seed carried all potency for new life. Under adverse conditions, the seed was damaged, and instead of reproducing male human perfection, it produced a misbegotten male, or a female. Women's ontological inferior humanity extended to her soul, reasoning, and will, which led Aquinas to a host of gender-based conclusions, some of which still pertain: For instance, women may not be ordained, since priesthood signifies the eminence of Christ, which females do not signify in their humanity; women should not preach, since this is an exercise of wisdom and authority of which they are not capable; and so on. If woman is redeemable, it is only through male mediation, that is, through Christ, marriage, and male priests. *Summa Theologica* 1, q. 92, a. 1, ad. 1.

21. "Post-Christian" Feminism and the Fatherhood of God, *Crux* (March 2000): 16.

oriented the life of the church as a new creation that was radically distinct from the world.

Because by the grace of God I grew up in a family and in church traditions to which such oppressive attitudes were foreign, I have only lately become aware of the kinds of theological issues that have left women feeling bereft of their true Spirit-filled humanity in Christ, resulting in what I believe is one of the most difficult moments of reckoning in the church—to respond in a truly Christian and cruciform manner to the challenge of feminist theology. I say this not to discount certain invaluable insights raised by women in this context. Far from it. The church has cause to repent and to take into account why these theologies exist and why evangelical women and others on the margins find points of commonality with their concerns. No, the real challenge to repentance stems from the fact that Christian theology, as the expression of our corporate *imago Dei* in Christ lived for the other "as better than ourselves" (Phil. 2:1–8),[22] ought to have made the issues that have birthed feminist theology utterly obsolete, even nonexistent, in the new creation.

But such attitudes do exist in our tradition, often couched in language of functional rather than ontological subordination. We argue about women's roles in the life of the church in relation to men, so that what began as impartial Spirit-gifting returns to the "law" of sexual bias. We must recognize the degree to which this is a result of not living as restored *imago Dei* in the Christ who has redeemed both men and women in his image and given his Spirit equally without measure or distinction. Such acts of Christ simply negate any relational or functional hierarchy, or favoritism, or sense of ontological superiority, or claims to Spirit-gifting based on gender rather than on God's freedom.

22. "If you have any encouragement from *being united with Christ,* if any comfort from *his love,* if *any fellowship with the Spirit,* if any *tenderness and compassion,* then make my joy complete by *being like-minded, having the same love, being one in spirit and purpose. Do nothing out of selfish ambition or vain conceit, but in humility consider others better than yourselves.* Each of you should look not only to your own interests, but also to the interests of *others. Your attitude should be the same as that of Christ Jesus:* Who, being in very nature God, did not consider equality with God something to be grasped, but made himself nothing, *taking the very nature of a servant,* being made in human likeness. And being found in appearance as a man, he humbled himself and became obedient to death—even death on a cross!" (emphasis added).

To be saved is to be reconstituted as human beings, and to be human is to be sexually differentiated. Thus, our life as the new creation in the restored *imago Dei* must essentially be an equally co-human relation of ontological unity-in-distinction—*ʾādām* as male and female in the likeness of God (Gen. 5:2) subsequently transformed by the new Adam (Romans 5; 8)—in the image of the Triune God.[23]

The Incarnation: God's Great Yes to Humanity in the Final Consummation of Creation

In conclusion, I would like to emphasize one more aspect of being made in the image of the true *human being*, Jesus Christ, that seems to have tremendous bearing on the reality of men and women living as sexual, bodily human beings in relation to and for one another. If, as stated above, to be a human being is to be sexually differentiated, then to *be saved* means that we *continue* to be female and male human beings in the age to come as new creations in Christ.[24] While the first statement may go undisputed, I'm not so sure about the second. Throughout periods of Christian history and among certain Christians

23. Using the term "equal" here, I am thinking not in a Western sense of "equal rights" but of the language in the Athanasian Creed: "And in this trinity there is nothing before or after, nothing greater or less, but all three persons are coeternal with each other and coequal. Thus in all things . . . both Trinity in unity and unity in Trinity must be worshipped. And he who desired to be saved should think thus of the Trinity" (John Leith, ed., *Creeds of the Church* [Louisville: John Knox, 1982], 706).

24. I am limiting my discussion in this paper to sexual differentiation rather than gender, which is at least in part a socially constructed concept. The question was raised at the conference whether there is gender in the new creation. This would make for an interesting discussion, one, however, that is not under the purview of this paper. My own initial thoughts, however, run in this direction: There is in Christ one ontological source and norm for humanity in all its variety, distinction, and relationality. If gender is "constructed" in part by "cultural" values and behaviors, then the "culture" of the new creation is shaped by the person of Christ and the values of the kingdom. "Gender" would have to be redefined according to this reality "contructed" by the Spirit so that sexual distinction *dictates* nothing but is rather an aspect of celebrated uniqueness within the fellowship of believers. For a fine discussion of feminist gender issues and life *in Christ*, see Woodhead, "God, Gender, and Identity."

today, life in the new creation carries a disembodied sense. The emphasis is on the saving of souls, not on *being saved* as the new creation.[25] Our created humanity—to be *ʾādām* as male and female—somehow gets blurred or even disregarded.[26]

This was brought home to me a few years ago as I was doing some work in feminist theology. On two separate occasions that took place within weeks of one another, I had conversations with two male friends of mine, both church leaders. Each of them asked me why it was so important to feminists to have female language for God that reflected their own humanity in God's image?[27] After all, said both men, there was neither sexuality in God *nor sexual distinction in the new creation.* Each man defended his point from Luke 20:34–36. I was in full agreement with the first statement and with it the understanding that our primary identity as *imago Dei* is neither sexual nor gendered.[28] However, I was stunned by the second and with the attempt to defend it scripturally from a passage in which Jesus is defending *bodily human resurrection.*

I responded by noting that in this passage Luke records Jesus as saying that "those who are considered worthy of taking part in that age and in the resurrection from the dead will neither marry nor be given in marriage" (v. 35), for, like the angels, they will no longer die and thus, assumedly, no longer procreate. There is no hint that they will cease to *be* human. Furthermore, Jesus goes on to say that "they are God's children, since they are children of the resurrection" (v. 36b). The suggestion is that those "children" who will live in the

25. English translations of life *kata sarka*—as lived according to "the flesh" or "the sinful nature"—do not help much in combating the dualism that denigrates creation and, in particular, human sexuality. I would argue that this is *not* what Paul is driving at when he speaks of life *kata sarka* or *kata pneuma* based on the Spirit-led, obedient, and utterly cruciform humanity of Jesus Christ.

26. In 1 Corinthians 6:12–17, Paul corrects the Corinthian misunderstanding at this point, as they attempt to realize fully their eschatological hope and thus ignore what Jesus' own life affirms—that they are bodily human temples of the Spirit in the world, both individually and corporately. See Fee, *First Epistle to the Corinthians*, 249–357.

27. Both of these men acknowledged, however, that part of their discomfort with feminist God-talk went beyond its being non-Christian. They recognized that the application of a different set of pronouns to God challenged their own self-identity as *men* in relation to the "quite male" God of their Christian imagination. At this point, they had answered their own question.

28. Woodhead, "God, Gender, and Identity," is excellent here.

age to come will share in Jesus' own *bodily* resurrection. Morever, these "children of God," whose identity is grounded in the covenanting God of Abraham, Isaac, and Jacob (whom Jesus is now introducing as *"Abba"!*), are precisely those *human* children made in his image and with whom his presence had historically dwelt.[29]

In short, a human resurrection requires a human (thus, sexually differentiated) body. The crucified Jesus did not resurrect as an androgyne, or an angel, or something else entirely. He rose a new *man*. His resurrected *body* was transformed within the continuity of creation. People experienced him in some recognizably "male" fashion after his resurrection in his walking, eating, natural-law-defying "spiritual" body, not as an immaterial spirit but as an eschatologically transformed human being with a body fit for the age to come.

Holding unswervingly to a Chalcedonian view of Jesus' divine-human life, I emphasize Jesus' humanity at this point to steer clear of a docetic tendency that surfaces in evangelicalism—one that fails to take Jesus' humanity seriously, making him mostly God and a little bit man, which not only empties of any meaning his temptation in the desert, his gut-wrenching appeal in Gethsemane, his cry of utter despair on the cross, and every human joy and hardship in between but also excuses us from taking seriously the call upon each of us to be like him in every way. This resemblance is to include his cruciform life and his radical relational reorientation of relationships, divine and human. Just as there is no dualism between the spiritual and the physical effects of sin, so there is none in redemption in Christ. Our "souls" are not saved; rather, *we* are. "If anyone is in Christ," says Paul, "he is a new creation; the old has gone, the new has come!" (2 Cor. 5:17)—including our humanity and the manner in which it lives out its new existence.[30]

29. Only now it is not by natural descent or human decision or action that they are the children of God. Jesus gives them the right, and they are subsequently born of water and the Spirit (John 1:12–13; 3:5).

30. This, notes Michael Gorman, is the language of prophetic fulfillment. As forgiven and justified people, Jews and Gentiles, slaves and free, men and women form the new Israel of God (Gal. 6:16), the people of his presence and the embodiment of the new creation. What God intended from the beginning (creation), what humans marred and what God will bring to future completion, has already broken into human history and life (new creation) (*Cruciformity*, 354).

I also emphasize his humanity to stress the ongoing reality of his human existence as the eternal Son. Our humanity really is hidden with Christ's humanity in God. As the firstborn from among the dead, Jesus takes his perfect humanity into God and keeps it there. Peter testifies to this reality at Pentecost; from his place of exaltation at the right hand of his Father, Jesus, still on the side of creation, gives the promised Spirit to all those whose lives are "crucified" and submitted to him as Lord, now sharing in the perfect *imago Dei* of the new creation (Acts 2:14–36).[31] His acts of entering into creation, being found in human likeness, and taking the form of a servant have everything to do with saving us and making us who and what we truly are.

Returning to the conversations with my two friends, I asked them why, if Jesus' incarnation was and remains the great embodied yes to creation and specifically to humanity, were they so quick to discount that as an *eternal* reality—the very mystery Paul attempts to describe in 1 Corinthians 15? Did they not look forward to being made new men, as I looked forward to being a new woman, each fully restored so that we could finally love one another selflessly and transparently? Both men were honest in their responses. One had always pictured himself in heaven as himself (male) but in order not to worry about lust had simply tried not to think about women being there *as women* and in his mind's eye had changed them into sexless beings. The other man's marriage was so unhappy that he simply did not want to entertain the prospect of being in eternal relation with his wife.

My friends are not unusual, except perhaps in their honesty. And yet where in the midst of such pain and bondage is the hope of being a *new creation* in Christ, finally made perfect in the image of the true human, Jesus Christ? How do we live out this ontological reality within the bodily limitations, urges, identities, and so on that we experience as human males and fe-

31. In reference to Psalm 8, the author of Hebrews makes clear in talking about Jesus' priestly human suffering and self-sacrifice and his exaltation as Son who also continues in his priestly role as the new human that he did not become some other kind of spiritual being, like an angel, nor will we. He who was made lower than the angels and was then exalted above them entered into every detail of human life, bringing it into realignment and proper relational direction toward obedience and self-giving sacrifice (Heb. 2:9–10).

males? And how do we live as sexual beings *together* in a way that bears the restored image of selflessly being for one another and glorifying God in the process? These are questions that must be answered in light of the cruciform life of Jesus Christ, who, tempted in every way as we are, submitted himself every day to the will of the Father and the power of the Spirit in constant prayer and worship. There are no easy answers. There is only cruciform life lived fully for the good and out of love for the other.

Salvation includes our reality as the church, of which Christ is the head or life-source, held together in all our distinctiveness by the creating, transforming Spirit and the unity of one Lord, one faith, one baptism, and one Father of us all (Eph. 4:5–6). We must learn to hear the urgency in Paul's words to the church in Corinth as he forbids divisions based on human distinctions, particularly sexuality, shaped by old values that represent neither the kingdom of God nor the body of Christ: "Don't you know that you yourselves are God's temple and that God's Spirit lives in you? If anyone destroys God's temple, God will destroy him; for God's temple is sacred, and you are that temple. Do not deceive yourselves. . . . All things are yours, whether Paul or Apollos or Cephas or the world or life or death or the present or the future—all are yours." Why? Because, says Paul, "you are of Christ, and Christ is of God" (1 Cor. 3:16–18, 21–23). There is no being saved, in fact, there is no being at all, apart from this incredible, radical reality. The question therefore becomes, Do we look like who, and whose, we are?

6

Salvation as Life
in the (New) City

Amy L. Sherman

Salvation Is "For"

It is not unusual for evangelicals to speak in terms of what
we are saved *from*. We are saved from our sins, from Satan,
from judgment and the wrath to come.

Salvation is indeed a rescue from all these things. And thank
God for such a rescue! But we are also saved *for;* there is a future aspect to our salvation. At the end of the Nicene Creed, we
recite: "And we look for the resurrection of the body, *and the life
of the world to come."*

For believers, salvation is past, present, and future. In history, there was a moment when we became Christ's own and
were transferred from the kingdom of darkness into the kingdom of the Son (Col. 1:13). Today, we are saved—the Good
News of grace that justified us is working sanctification in us
presently; today, united with Christ, God's justice smiles upon
us. Today, in some mysterious way, we are "seated . . . in the
heavenly realms in Christ Jesus" (Eph. 2:6). But a day of salva-

tion—a future day—is also coming. It is a rescue from the final judgment (1 Thess. 1:10), for we were not appointed "to suffer wrath but to receive salvation" (1 Thess. 5:9). We are waiting to possess our full inheritance (1 Peter 1:4). We are waiting for full entry into "the life that is truly life" (1 Tim. 6:19). We are waiting to enter into all that God has for us in the future Sabbath rest (Heb. 4:9–11). We are looking forward to our life in the world to come. In this sense, salvation is future.

The World to Come

The purposes of our salvation are many and varied. In the little Book of Ephesians alone, we learn of several. We are saved in order that we will be "holy and blameless in his sight" (1:4) and that we will "grow up into him who is the Head, that is, Christ" (4:15). Primarily, we are saved to glorify God: "In him we were also chosen . . . in order that we, who were the first to hope in Christ, might be for the praise of his glory" (1:11–12). We are saved to do good works that God prepared in advance for us to do (2:10). Part of the purpose of our salvation through the cross is for Jesus to create "in himself one new man out of the two" (2:15); we are, in other words, apparently saved to pursue a full reconciliation among men.

But we are also saved for the purpose of enjoying what our generous God wants to give us: eternal life in the world to come. Paul prays that the Ephesians will meditate on this aspect of their salvation, that they will "know the hope to which he has called [them], the riches of his glorious inheritance in the saints" (1:18). Paul wants the Ephesians to know that God saved them in order to seat them in the heavenly realms so that "in the coming ages he might show [them] the incomparable riches of his grace, expressed in his kindness to [them] in Christ Jesus" (2:7).

Yet this "world to come" is, for too many Christians, rather vague in content. Surely we desire to go to heaven and not to that other place. And surely we know that heaven will be better than this place. Yet lingering in the hearts of some—and perhaps especially in ours as rich North Americans (relative to the world, we are among the extremely wealthy)—are nagging questions about this future life. We have fears that we are embarrassed to vocalize because they do not sound very Christian. But they are there: "Will heaven be, well, *boring?* Won't I get tired of floating around in the clouds in my white robe, playing my harp?"

Popular culture, with its angel pins and pictures of puffy clouds, perpetuate these unspoken worries. But Scripture gives us wonderfully concrete visions of the life of the world to come—not highly detailed portraits, to be sure, but much more information than we often have in our truncated imaginations.

Most importantly, we are told that what is coming is "a new heaven and a new earth." We are told that a "new city" is coming. This language is intentional and crucial. We are spoken to in words we understand, words that have correspondence to realities we can see and experience. We are not told that what is coming is a new "clobuzey" or a new "hanamayatopa"—a foreign word, a "totally other" reality we can never wrap our heads around. None of us is certain what the new earth or the new city will look like exactly, but we do know what the words *earth* and *city* mean. They have content for us. We have reference points for such terms. What is to come is something grand and glorious and something that has a degree of correspondence to the world we now know.

C. S. Lewis captures this well in the last book of the delightful Narnia series. In *The Last Battle,* the old Narnia (corresponding to the old earth) has been consumed, and the new Narnia (i.e., the new earth) has come. The two are not unlike in essential respects, yet the new far surpasses the old:

> It is as hard to explain how this sunlit land was different from the old Narnia, as it would be to tell you how the fruits of that country taste. Perhaps you will get some idea of it, if you think like this. You may have been in a room in which there was a window that looked out on a lovely bay of the sea or a green valley that wound away among the mountains. And in the wall of that room opposite to the window there may have been a looking glass. And the sea in the mirror, or the valley in the mirror, were in one sense just the same as the real ones; yet at the same time they were somehow different—deeper, more wonderful, more like places in a story: in a story you have never heard but very much want to know. The difference between the old Narnia and the new Narnia was like that. The new one was a deeper country:

every rock and flower and blade of grass looked as if it meant
more. I can't describe it any better than that: if you ever get
there, you will know what I mean.[1]

If we consider the words of the Lord's Prayer in Matthew
6:9–13, we get a clue that it is important to God that we understand these realities. After all, we petition our heavenly Father:
"Thy kingdom come, thy will be done *on earth as it is in heaven.*"
We are, in effect, saying, "Father, let heaven come down to
earth. So transform life on earth that it imitates life in heaven.
So infuse the earth with heavenly realities and heavenly ways
that it becomes, essentially, heavenly." And this is precisely
what happens in the eschaton: Heaven comes down to earth.
Consider Revelation 21:1–2: "Then I saw a new heaven and a
new earth, for the first heaven and the first earth had passed
away, and there was no longer any sea. I saw the Holy City, the
new Jerusalem, *coming down out of heaven.*"

Tim Keller of Redeemer Presbyterian Church in New York
City has noted that this is one of the unique points of Christianity compared to other world religions. In Christianity, heaven
comes down to earth.[2] We do not fully comprehend these
things, and our tendencies to look upward when we think of
heaven and to think of the dead "rising" and ascending to
heaven have biblical warrant (consider Christ's ascension in
Acts 1). But the picture we are given in the Book of Revelation
underscores the concreteness of what will happen in the final
days. We will not go up to some unknown destination; rather, a
new city will come down to us.

Characteristics of the New City

A full understanding (and appreciation) of the salvation we
have been granted requires that we grasp to the fullest measure
the content God has shared with us in his Word regarding the
life of the world to come. Our passion for heaven should increase as our comprehension of it deepens. The first step in this

1. *The Last Battle* (New York: Collier Books, 1956), 170–71.
2. Tim Keller, "Lord of the City" (sermon preached at Redeemer Presbyterian Church, New York City, 7 January 2001).

process is recognizing that heaven will not be "totally other," some unimaginable and foreign mystery, but rather a fully restored and remade creation. We have, in short, a jumping-off point for our imaginations. We can gaze at the majestic Swiss Alps on a clear, sunny, seventy-five-degree day, filled with joy and awe, and say, "In heaven, there will be beauty like this—but a far more gloriously beautiful beauty."

We have additional content in the image of the New City. We could rewrite the end of the Nicene Creed to say, "and we look forward to life in the New City."

Now, as someone who lives and works in the inner city, there is a degree to which this is a turnoff to me. When I go on vacation, I do not go to cities. I go to national parks. I go to Lake Tahoe. I hope someday to go to Banff. "City" conjures up traffic and noise and pollution and crime and alienation and coldness. We often fear the city; we can see it as a place of violence, a place of strife, a place of dog-eat-dog. I am not excited about an eternal vacation in Chicago!

But our ultimate destination as followers of Christ is a city. The ultimate destination of all of history is a city. We began in a garden in Genesis, but we end in a city in Revelation 22. This is God's plan, and so it must be good and glorious. Therefore, we need to reconstruct our understanding of "city." Scripture helps us here. The Bible reveals at least four beautiful characteristics of the city.[3]

The City Is a Refuge for the Weak

First, the city is a refuge for the weak. Tim Keller has noted that cities are gifts from God. Their population densities provide the weak with a refuge. Immigrants, for example, tend to go to cities because they can gather with kinsmen and feel strength in numbers. Minorities and society's "alternative" citizens (punk rockers, homosexuals, Bohemian types) are likely to live in cities because, again, they can build mini-communities there. They can find and live among others like themselves rather than being the "odd men out" in a small town. Frequently, city residents do not think of such people as weird, for

3. I am indebted to Tim Keller for some of these observations.

in a sense one expects to see "strange" people in cities. And so the offbeat, the different, the unconventional can live more comfortably in cities than they would in a small town or rural village.

In the Old Testament, cities were places of refuge. Indeed, six were established specifically as "cities of refuge," three east of the Jordan River and three west of it. In ancient times, outside the city meant wilderness; beyond the city walls was frontier. There, frontier "justice" reigned—the rule of the strong, the rule of individuals taking into their own hands the right of punishment. But God's law provided for rural dwellers who accidentally and without malice killed someone. In such an instance, the guilty one could flee to a city of refuge and there be ensured of a trial. He could obtain city justice—the rule of law—instead of facing frontier vengeance (i.e., being slain by a kinsman of the person he had accidentally killed). Inside the city, in short, he could enjoy the benefits of "civilization." (As Keller points out, the word *civilization* has its roots in the Latin word for city.)

The city, then, understood in this context, is a place of safety, a place of security. The biblical pictures of the New Jerusalem highlight this characteristic. Revelation 21:12–14 speaks of the high wall that surrounds the city, of its twelve strong gates and twelve foundations. This language is meant to generate within us a sense that this city is protected, strong, unshakeable. In Isaiah 54:11–14, we see a similar picture of the New Jerusalem and are comforted by the words in verse 14: "In righteousness you will be established: Tyranny will be far from you; you will have nothing to fear. Terror will be far removed; it will not come near you." Thus, Isaiah can prophesy to the people, "Great will be your children's peace" (v. 13).

One of the glories of our life to come in the New City is that it will be a fear-free life. This has come to mean a great deal to me in the wake of the September 11 terrorist attacks in New York City and Washington, D.C. I know now with much more force that these cities are not places where "terror will be far removed." The hope of life in the New City has become more precious to me, for there we will live in a safe place, a place of security, a place of refuge.

The City Is a Place of Permanent Residency

Second, life in the New City will be a wonderful life because we will have a permanent home there, a permanent residency. In the letters to the seven churches in the early chapters of Revelation, the apostle John typically reports that each church is commended by Jesus, then corrected by him, exhorted, and promised rewards for faithfulness. The letter to the church in Philadelphia is notable because for this body of believers the Lord Jesus has only words of commendation. Their discipleship is, among all the churches, the most faithful. The reward promised by Christ to the Philadelphians is: "Him who overcomes I will make a pillar in the temple of my God. Never again will he leave it" (Rev. 3:12).

Commentator Edward McDowell reminds us that such words would have been of particular comfort to the believers at Philadelphia, because their city had been wracked by earthquakes.[4] Fearing the aftershocks, many residents had moved out of the city and were living in mean huts, precarious, impermanent quarters. By contrast, in the New City, they will be a "pillar" in the temple of God—strong, unshakeable—and they will remain in that temple eternally, never having to leave. There is a solid home for the Philadelphians and for us. It is the "city with foundations" to which Abraham, living on earth in tents, looked forward (Heb. 11:9–12).

Ours is a fast-paced and mobile culture. We often move. More and more frequently, family members are scattered, living apart from one another. Our sense of community is transient, as old friends leave us. Many ache for rootedness. In such a setting, our longing for a home is unfulfilled. Part of the good news of our salvation is that what awaits us in the New City is permanent residency, a home we will never have to leave. In the New Jerusalem, there will be not only no tears and no suffering but also no good-byes.

The City Is the Place Where We Are Named

Third, the city is the place where we will receive a new name. The promise made to the believers at Philadelphia continues in

4. *The Meaning and Message of the Book of Revelation* (Nashville: Broadman, 1951), 57–58.

Revelation 3:12: "I will write on him the name of my God and the name of the city of my God, the new Jerusalem, which is coming down out of heaven from my God; and I will also write on him my new name." As we consider this promise, it is helpful to note a similar word from Revelation 22:4, written about us as dwellers in the New City: "They will see his [Jesus'] face, and his name will be on their foreheads."

In the New Jerusalem, we will be people who have been named. Keller notes that the full significance of this truth is highlighted when we consider it against the backdrop of the story of the Tower of Babel in Genesis 11:1–9. Keller explains that part of the sin of those at Babel was that they wanted to make a name for themselves ("Come, let us build for ourselves a city, with a tower that reaches to the heavens, so that we may make a name for ourselves" [v. 4]).

The desire for reputation is a root of many evils in human cities. To make a name for ourselves means achieving respect or admiration in the eyes of others. It means "making it to the top." It means building our own securities—whether by acquiring wealth or power or fame or status. Making a name for ourselves is a human-centered and self-centered activity. We ache to matter, to count, to be considered special. We must prove ourselves; we must impress. To do so, we are often willing to harm others along the way. We raise ourselves up by putting others down. Competition becomes cutthroat. Worthy pursuits are cast aside so that all attention, energy, and drive can be focused on the goal of building our reputations. It is an exhausting quest and often an elusive one. Consider the athlete who has finally broken the world record. The name he has made for himself—"world's fastest runner"—will soon be taken away by a better, faster sprinter.

Into this frenetic activity, God speaks: "Child, *I* will give you your name."

In the New City, we are freed from our senseless quest. We are named. We matter because the God of the universe has purchased us for himself and has called us his own. The focus needs no longer be on our exhausting activity—strivings that are always incomplete because we simply lack the strength to create on our own the sense of purpose for which we long. We are weak. God knows this and commands our activities to cease; we passively receive from him. We are given a name as his gift to us. He knows that we, like the Christians at Philadelphia, "have little strength" (Rev. 3:8). He invites us to rest in the liberty of his naming us rather than foolishly attempting to name ourselves.

The idea that Jesus' name will be written on our foreheads implies further that we belong to him. The picture reminds me of what we do with the little children in our urban ministry's summer camp program. Each child is assigned to an adult counselor for the week. The child's name tag has his or her own name written on it in big letters, but the name tag also contains the name of his or her counselor. That way, if a child gets separated from his or her group, a staff person or volunteer can examine the name tag and know to which counselor the child belongs. The child has a place, a caretaker. So do we. Our heavenly name tags include not only our names (for in Christianity, personality extends into eternity) but also the phrase "belongs to Jesus."

Yet the name we receive secures not only our belonging. The name of Jesus written on our foreheads assures our security, our protection. A holy and just God looks on us and sees us as his own Son's possessions. Jesus' name serves as a protective covering. The wrath of God will not touch those who have the Son's name engraved on them.

Moreover, Revelation 3 tells us that the name of the New City of God will be written on us. Our identity will be as "Jerusalemites" (just as now my geographic residency names me, in the eyes of the world, a "Virginian" or an "American"). This reinforces the notion of permanent residency noted earlier. This side of heaven, the name written on us is "alien" and "stranger." Like Abraham, we have no abiding city. Like Abraham, we are "longing for a better country—a heavenly one" (Heb. 11:16). To the extent that we are faithful to our Christian identity, we ought not to feel at home in our culture. We ought to feel the distresses and discomfort an alien feels in a strange land. These sufferings will not last forever, though; the promise for us is that one day we will no longer be aliens but permanent citizens of our true homeland.

In the New City We See Jesus Face to Face

A secure refuge. A permanent residence. A name and a belonging. All are incredible benefits of our salvation. But the greatest feature of life in the New City is that in its center Jesus reigns. *And we shall see him.*

This is the pinnacle of our intimacy with God. We regain what was lost in Genesis 3. In the Garden, we were separated from God's presence. Yet throughout redemptive history, he has been pursuing us, and he is restoring his presence in incremental installments.[5] We see him dimly in the smoking firepot of Genesis 15. Jacob feels his grip at Peniel (Gen. 32:30). I AM is in the burning bush in Exodus 3. He is present in the pillar of fire in Exodus 13 and in the tabernacle in Exodus 25. Then he puts his name in the temple Solomon builds (1 Kings 9:3), and God's people can meet him there. But this is still not the communion we are intended to have.

And so comes, in the words of Rev. Greg Thompson, the "earth-shattering words of the first chapter of John: 'The Word became flesh and tabernacled among us.'"[6] God reveals himself in the face of Jesus. God draws near in Christ. Here, though, the glory is veiled in the flesh. The disciples on the Mount of Transfiguration cannot gaze upon Christ in his full glory because of the burning of his light. Yet the progression of restored fellowship marches on. God comes ever nearer. We discover in 1 Corinthians 3 that *we* are now the temple of God; God inhabits us by his Spirit. Paul speaks in Colossians of Christ *in* us, the hope of glory (1:27). Still, this is by faith and not by sight. At the end of our journey, however, faith will give way to sight. In the New City, we will behold his face—in all his glory—with our very eyes. To quote Thompson:

> The face that was hidden from Moses, the face that David longed to see in Psalm 27, will now be revealed to you, and you will know it as the face of your dearest love. The face that would have brought death to Moses had he seen it when he asked in Exodus 33 now brings hope and life. God's presence is at last restored to

5. Greg Thompson, "Strength for Today, Hope for Tomorrow" (sermon preached at Trinity Presbyterian Church, Charlottesville, Virginia, 12 August 2001).
6. Ibid.

his people. This is the ocean fullness into which the entire river of the biblical narrative is flowing. This is the whole point—that God's people will be restored to him and that he will be restored to them.[7]

This One we will see face to face in the New City is our bridegroom, and we will be, *experientially,* his bride. We have been *called* his bride all along, but now the wedding feast has come. Now every impurity has been burned away from us; now his sanctifying labors are finished. Now we enjoy complete union with him, untouched, untroubled by the stain of our sinfulness.

And now—amazingly—we partner with our bridegroom in his rule of the universe. In the New City, we are the overcomers who receive the promise of Revelation 3:21, namely, the right to sit with Jesus on his throne. We receive the promise of Revelation 2:26, namely, to have authority over the nations. Consider the words in the song that the four living creatures of Revelation 5 sing to the Lamb about *us,* the ones Jesus has purchased with his blood: "You have made them to be a kingdom and priests to serve our God, *and they will reign on the earth*" (v. 10, emphasis added).

Is heaven boring? Only if seeing God face to face is boring; only if enjoying eternal marriage and partnership with Jesus is boring; only if reigning on earth is boring. The privileges that await us are breathtaking and mind-boggling.

Application

Why is knowing this so important? Because we need to have *content* for our hope. We must be disabused of the nebulous and faintly unsatisfying half-formed ideas we have of heaven and eternal life. A fuller understanding of salvation as life in the New City will enable us to live in a new way here: to live backward and to live forward.

By living backward, I mean living now as foretastes of the realities of the consummated kingdom that is to come. A guest preacher at my church once told us about a dire conflict in his

7. Ibid.

marriage. It centered on the "preview controversy." You know, the old argument that occurs when you get a video home from Blockbuster and have to decide whether to watch the previews. The guest preacher said he represents the pro-preview perspective; he wants to watch all the previews so that he knows what the coming attractions are. His wife represents the anti-preview faction; she thinks they are a waste of time. She's got other things to do, phone calls to make, letters to write, and just wants to be called in when the screen reads, "And now for our feature presentation." The preacher went on to argue that his perspective is a decidedly more biblical one. I would have to agree.

The Bible is all about previews of coming attractions. The "feature film" is the kingdom of God in all its glory, beauty, and wholeness, and there are previews of it throughout the Old Testament. The Old Testament provides prophetic glimpses into what life in the feature film—or the New City—will be like. In Psalm 46:9, for example, God says that one day he will make wars cease to the ends of the earth: He will break the bow and shatter the spear. Psalm 72 gives a preview of life under the reign of King Jesus, the King whom God will endow with justice: "He will judge your people in righteousness, your afflicted ones with justice. The mountains will bring prosperity to the people, the hills the fruit of righteousness. He will defend the afflicted among the people and save the children of the needy" (vv. 2–4).

Or consider the preview presented in Isaiah 32:1–5:

> See, a king will reign in righteousness and rulers will rule with justice. Each man will be like a shelter from the wind and a refuge from the storm, like streams of water in the desert and the shadow of a great rock in a thirsty land. Then the eyes of those who see will no longer be closed, and the ears of those who hear will listen. The mind of the rash will know and understand, and the stammering tongue will be fluent and clear. No longer will the fool be called noble nor the scoundrel be highly respected.

There are so many previews of the time that is to come when swords will be beaten into plowshares, when the child will play safely at the viper's nest, when the lion will lie down with the lamb, when every man will rest secure under his own vine and fig tree, when the desert will blossom with crocus, when the burning sand will become a pool, when the mute tongue will be loosed and the lame will leap like a deer.

We know many characteristics of life in the New City, in the consummated kingdom of God. It is a place of peace, justice, love, mercy, wholeness, reconciled relationships, sufficiency, and unity amid diversity (one community, yet composed of every tribe, tongue, and language). During his ministry on earth, Jesus offered people foretastes of these realities. He announced that the kingdom of God had arrived, had broken into this world. And as the Christmas song "Joy to the World" celebrates, Jesus began to "make his blessings known far as the curse is found." His actions destroyed the works of the devil (1 John 3:8) and rolled back the curse. When Jesus was performing his miracles, he was doing more than merely healing individual sufferers. He was reaching into the future, fully consummated kingdom of God and yanking a foretaste of it back into the present. It was as if he were announcing, "In the feature film, there will be no blindness, and so I give you your sight, blind Bartimaeus. In my Father's kingdom, there will be no leprosy, and so I touch the lepers now and make them clean. In the New City, there will be no death, and so I say to you, 'Lazarus, up from the grave!'"

As followers of Jesus, we should seek to live as foretastes of the consummated kingdom. Our corporate fellowship ought to be marked by the values, priorities, and mores of the kingdom so that when nonbelievers experience our fellowship, they savor a foretaste of life in the New City. We cannot be foretastes of something that we do not know; we cannot be a preview of something for which we have no content. That is why it is imperative that we grasp what life in the New City is all about.

We also need to understand the life of the world to come to live forward. By this, I mean living a life over which this banner could be strung: "Risking Now for Lasting Joy." Our hearts need to be captured by the future promise, the future inheritance, held out for us. This, the Book of Hebrews teaches, is what enabled Abraham's sacrificial faith and bold risk-taking:

> By faith Abraham, when called to go to a place he would later receive as his inheritance, obeyed and went, even though he did

not know where he was going. By faith he made his home in the promised land like a stranger in a foreign country; he lived in tents, as did Isaac and Jacob, who were heirs with him of the same promise. *For he was looking forward to the city with foundations, whose architect and builder is God.*

11:8–10, emphasis added

Abraham looked forward, saw the New City as his future inheritance, and lived an earthly life of radical faith and costly obedience. He saw lasting joy in the future; it enabled amazing risk-taking in the present.

John Piper has commented on this dynamic in the Christian life:

> If somebody falls out of an airplane with no parachute on and you don't have one either, you aren't going to jump out after them. It won't do any good. Two deaths aren't better than one. But if you have a parachute on, you might just try one of those awesome rescue attempts, and free fall like a bullet to catch the helpless and pull your cord. It's the hope of safety in the end that releases radical, sacrificial love now.[8]

The apostle Paul believed in and witnessed this powerful dynamic. He says of the Colossian Christians, "We have heard of . . . the love you have for all the saints—the faith and love that spring from *the hope that is stored up for you in heaven*" (Col. 1:4–5, emphasis added). If we do not know, if we do not study, if we do not meditate on the hope laid up for us in heaven, we will lack this important source of power that will help us lay down our lives now in love for God and neighbor.

Conclusion: Salt of the Earth

In this life, we have a calling from our Lord to be the salt of the earth. We see a picture—one rich with kingdom overtones—of what this looks like in 2 Kings 2:19–22. It is the account of the prophet Elisha and the healing of the waters at Jericho:

8. "God's Invincible Purpose, Foundations for Full Assurance: Behold I Make All Things New" (sermon preached at Bethlehem Baptist Church, Minneapolis, Minnesota, 26 April 1992).

The men of the city said to Elisha, "Look, our lord, this town is well situated, as you can see, but the water is bad and the land is unproductive." "Bring me a new bowl," he said, "and put salt in it." So they brought it to him. Then he went out to the spring and threw the salt into it, saying, "This is what the LORD says: 'I have healed this water. Never again will it cause death or make the land unproductive.'" And the water has remained wholesome to this day, according to the word Elisha had spoken.

To grasp the full significance of the story, we must remember that this miracle occurred in Jericho. We recall Jericho, of course, from our Sunday school lessons about Joshua and the fall of the city wall. But what we probably forget is that after the "walls came-a tumblin' down," Joshua put a curse on this city.

The picture in 2 Kings 2, therefore, is of a river of death flowing into a cursed city. The water, we learn from the residents' report, is bad, harmful, unhealthy, polluted—it brought sickness and death and left the land barren. But Elisha performs a miracle. God tells him to throw salt in the water, and God, in his mercy, uses that salt to heal the water so that it becomes wholesome and life-giving.

Now consider Jesus' call for us to be the salt of the earth. Today, we have throughout our lands "rivers of death" flowing into our cities. There is a river of death flowing into the neighborhood in which I live. Drugs are flowing in; violence is flowing in; hopelessness, abuse, bondage, destitution are flowing in. But God can heal this river that brings barrenness and that destroys. It may be his plan to throw us—the salt of the earth—into that river. Right into the thick of it!

It is a scary proposition, for when salt hits water, it dissolves. We might say that the salt is "spent" in the water or that it gives up its life. This is self-sacrificing salt. This is behavior that risks.

But there is another picture—so closely related to the one in 2 Kings 2 that we must be meant to see the connection—that we can savor. It is from the final chapter of the Bible:

Then the angel showed me the river of the water of life, as clear as crystal, flowing from the throne of God and of the Lamb down the middle of the great street of the city. On each side of the river stood the tree of life, bearing twelve crops of fruit, yielding its fruit every month. And the leaves of the tree are for the healing of the nations. No longer will there be any curse.

Rev. 22:1–3

Here, in contrast to Jericho, the city under the curse, we have the New Jerusalem. Here, instead of the river of death, we have the water of life. Here we see the New City, where there is life and wholeness, where pollution and evil and death are banished.

This is our inheritance. With the knowledge that we will live there, we can be salt here.

7

Christians Should Be Converted Pagans

*The Apologetic Problem of a Gospel
That Denies Our Earthiness*

Loren Wilkinson

Christians often use the word *pagan* to describe the modern secular world and all its religious alternatives to acceptance of Jesus as Savior. This is made all the easier by an explicitly defined movement that is happy to be known as "pagan" or "neopagan." Lesslie Newbigin points out, in the opening pages of *Foolishness to the Greeks,* that such *post-Christian* paganism is considerably more resistant to the gospel than pre-Christian paganism. He is undoubtedly correct. But here we must proceed with caution, for it would be simple to conclude that such "post" (and the suffix usually implies "anti") Christian movements have considered the Christian message of salvation and rejected it and thus are, to use the pungent Pauline phrase, "without excuse."

But the matter is not as simple as that, and the existence of contemporary neo-pagans, most of whom have some sort of Christian background, requires us to look more carefully at the word and at why so many who have explicitly rejected Christian faith in fact choose to be called pagan. Neo-paganism, I believe, is an attempt to recover an aspect of being human that is central to the gospel but is often obscured—that is, we cannot be fully human until our restored relationship with the Creator results in a restored relationship not only with other men and women but also with the rest of creation, which is seen and accepted as a divine gift. Paganism (old and new) sees that divine gift as the only essential revelation, and harmony with creation and its resident gods or spirits as the only salvation. Thus, paganism is forever inadequate for the wholeness its believers seek. But inasmuch as paganism does have open eyes to the gift-nature of creation, it glimpses a truth to which Christians are sometimes blind. Our culture is being tilted toward paganism as much by an inadequate understanding and modeling by Christians of the creational scope of salvation as by pagan perversity and hardness of heart.

Beneath the puerility and plain silliness of a good bit of neo-pagan ritual lies a longing for wholeness that can be fulfilled only through a reconciliation with the Creator, a reconciliation that cannot be achieved outside of what God has accomplished in Christ. The attempts by pagans old and new to achieve that reconciliation on their own through various attempts to participate in the rhythms of "nature" always fail, and such attempts were roundly and rightly condemned by the prophets. At the same time, paganism is not entirely mistaken, for however inadequate and incomplete it is, as Psalm 19 makes clear, creation does contain a message about the Creator. The voice of the heavens "goes out into all the earth, their words to the ends of the world" (v. 4). Paul echoes that affirmation in Romans 1: "Since the creation of the world God's invisible qualities . . . have been clearly seen, being understood from what has been made" (v. 20). Of course, Paul proceeds to draw from this universal revelation of God the conclusion that such pagan recognition of God in creation always ends in some form of idolatry. But the danger for Christians today is that we are so afraid of the possibility of paganism or pantheism that we radically distance Creator from creation and understand salvation in such a way that it has no implications for creation. Until our understanding and our living out of new life in Jesus Christ involve a changed relationship with the earth, which God is also making new, we encourage an unconverted paganism, for paganism, rightly understood, is not an alternative to belief in the Triune God but a preparation for it. A Christian who is not at the same time a redeemed pagan is in danger of a kind of Gnostic or Manichean denial of what it means to be a physical, created being enmeshed in the cycles of creation. Thus, Christians need to be converted pagans.

At this point we need to stop and reflect on the meaning of the word *pagan*. *Pagan* today is used in various ways and is a particularly good example of the semantics of that proto-deconstructionist Humpty Dumpty, who in Lewis Carroll's *Through the Looking Glass* pronounced, "When I use a word . . . it means just what I choose it to mean, neither more nor less." Let me begin by describing two contrasting uses of the word as a prelude to the way I am using the word (recalling, perhaps, Humpty Dumpty's further observation that "when I make a word do a lot of work . . . I always pay it extra").[1]

Paganism according to the Neo-Pagans

One of the things I do not mean when I say that Christians should be converted pagans is that they should be converted *neo*-pagans (though, of course, the reverse is true, and I hope that all who currently consider themselves neo-pagans will eventually come to know Christ). The neo-pagan movement is widespread in many parts of Europe and North America. It is an important part of that smorgasbord of spiritualities that has been spread on the postmodern table. The label "postmodern" is particularly apt when applied to neo-paganism, for the movement is clearly both a child of and a reaction against the sterility of the modern. This ambivalent relationship with modernity is evident in the fact that in a survey published in Margot Adler's definitive study of the movement called *Drawing Down the Moon,* by far the most common occupations of neo-pagan respondents were in computer-related fields. The possi-

---

1. Lewis Carroll, *The Annotated Alice: Alice's Adventures in Wonderland and Through the Looking Glass,* with an introduction and notes by Martin Gardner (New York: Clarkson N. Potter, 1960), 270.

ble reasons for this computer-assisted flourishing of neo-paganism is a fascinating study in itself that we cannot explore here. (My own suspicion is that neo-paganism is both a reaction against the sterility of the increasingly virtual modern world, which computers encourage, and at the same time a convincing technical substitute for magic.) In any case, one of the best places to sample neo-paganism's understanding of itself is to explore its various Web pages.

One defines a neo-pagan as:

> an individual whose interest in the religious sphere lies in patterns of belief which are non-orthodox and non-traditional in Western society and which more specifically pre-date Western society's dominant belief systems as represented, for example, by Christianity or Judaism.

The interesting thing about this definition is how little it says positively about the content of neo-paganism and how much it says about neo-paganism's nonorthodox, nontraditional, and pre-Christian nature. Another Web page definition is a bit more helpful, though it is still deeply colored by the need to distance neo-paganism from Christianity: "Modern pagans are people who follow nature-oriented religions or 'earth religions' (in contrast to conventional religions that stress the after-life)." This definition gets at the heart of the two main aspects of neo-paganism. First, it is a "nature-religion" or an "earth-religion"—that is, adherents seek salvation by means of honoring and participating in the cycles of nature. Second, it is an "earth-religion" in conscious contrast to what is perceived to be the explicitly "otherworldly" nature of "traditional religions"—and certainly Christianity is overwhelmingly the most common "traditional religion" in the backgrounds of neo-pagans. (Surveys suggest that roughly three-fourths of those who identify themselves as neo-pagans were raised in some form of Christianity.)[2]

2. In Margot Adler's survey of neo-pagan religious background, 23.5 percent said their background was Catholic, 9 percent Anglican or Episcopal, 39.2 percent Protestant, and 9 percent some mix of Catholic and Protestant. These results very closely match the results of another survey done by Gordon Melton, who found that 25.8 percent of neo-pagans surveyed said they had a Catholic background, and 42.7 percent said they were Protestant. The figures for a Jewish background were 6.2 and 9 percent, respectively. Margot Adler, *Drawing Down the Moon* (New York: Penguin, 1997), 445.

Selena Fox's statement of faith, "I Am Pagan," published on the Internet a few years ago, provides an excellent positive account of what neo-pagans believe. Fox declares:

> I am Pagan. I am a part of the whole of Nature. The Rocks, the Animals, the Plants, the Elements, and Stars are my relatives.
> . . .
> I am Pagan. I embrace Pantheism, acknowledging that the Divine is everywhere and in everything. I honour the Divine that is within the oak trees in the forest, in the herbs in the garden, in the wild birds singing in the trees, in the rock outcroppings on the hillside, in myself, and yes, even in "things" such as my car, cameras, and computers. I understand that everything with a physical body has a spiritual body, too. The physical and spiritual are deeply intertwined, not separate, in this world of form. I honour the interconnectedness of Creator and Creation.
> I am Pagan. I hear the cries of Mother Earth who is upset with the harm being done to the environment by humankind. I am dismayed by the pollution of the air, the soil, and the waters.
> I am Pagan. Nature Spirituality is my religion and my life's foundation. Nature is my spiritual teacher and holy book. I am part of nature, and nature is part of me. My understanding of Nature's inner mysteries grows as I journey on this spiritual path.[3]

"I Am Pagan" (of which this is only a brief part) is heavily influenced by the ideologies of the past few decades. It is also highly selective in what it affirms about nature. In reality, nature is far from gentle, and enthusiasm for "the natural" usually increases as people are distanced from its harshness. Nature alone (Wordsworth to the contrary) is at best an ambivalent spiritual teacher, and it contains much that is dark and cruel. So it would be easy to dismiss Fox's credo as suburban and politically correct posturing. But Christians should not miss the genuine longing for wholeness that lies behind it or fail to ask why that longing has gone unfulfilled by the Christian gospel.

One Internet definition of neo-paganism calls it "European native spirituality," which is a useful definition on several accounts. To begin with, it recognizes the deep appeal of "native spirituality"

3. Copies available from Selena Fox, Circle Sanctuary, Box 219, Mt. Horeb, WI 53572.

in North America, where there are still native communities that have direct links to their pre-Christian and pagan pasts.[4] A European of English, German, or Scandinavian descent faces obvious problems, however, with trying to find his or her spiritual roots in Kwakiutl, Sioux, or Ojibway culture. Thus, there has been an attempt to resurrect the pre-Christian paganisms of Northern Europe. The paganism of choice is "Celtic," but there is a smaller group seeking to recover or reinvent Norse religious practice. (As far as I know, there has been no serious attempt to recover the more widely known polytheistic paganism of Greece and Rome—though the names of those old gods show up frequently in neopagan ritual, which is unabashedly eclectic.)

All these movements, as I have suggested, can aptly be labeled "postmodern," and nowhere is this more evident than in their attitude toward the question of continuity of the beliefs with the historical pagan spiritualities they claim to follow. Ronald Hutton, in a series of books, has shown decisively that most of the claims for continuity with the Celtic past are largely wishful thinking, many based on nineteenth-century fabrications. In *The Pagan Religions of the Ancient British Isles,* Hutton concludes that "all told, the paganism of today has virtually nothing in common with that of the past except the name, which itself is of Christian coinage."[5]

Charlotte Allen, in a recent article titled "The Scholars and the Goddess," surveys the evidence for the central tenet of Wicca (which is perhaps the largest and most clearly defined "denomination" within paganism). The tenet states that the Mediterranean world was once dominated by matriarchal societies that worshiped a goddess closely associated with nature and that those peaceful matriarchies were wiped out by patriarchal cultures that worshiped a transcendent male deity. Allen's conclusion is that most of Wiccan belief is a "1950s concoction" and that there is "no indication, either archeological or in the written record, that any ancient people ever worshipped a single, archetypal goddess."[6]

4. In fact, the prevailing spirituality of most Native Americans is Christian—sometimes in some syncretistic synthesis with original tribal religion but more often in fairly radical tension with it.

5. *The Pagan Religions of the Ancient British Isles: Their Nature and Legacy* (Oxford: Blackwell, 1991), 337.

6. *The Atlantic Monthly* 288 (January 2001): 19.

The significant thing is that these abundant disproofs of a historical basis for neo-pagan belief have little impact on the neo-pagans. Starhawk, perhaps the best-known neo-pagan apologist, told Allen that "most of us look at the archeological artifacts and images as a source of art or beauty or something to speculate about, because the images fit with our theory that the earth is sacred, and that there is a cycle of birth and growth and regeneration."[7] Another Wicca practitioner, "Diotima Mantineia," said:

> It doesn't matter to me how old Wicca is, because . . . the Creator of this universe has been manifesting to us for all time, in the forms of gods and goddesses that we can relate to. This personal connection with Deity is what is meaningful.[8]

When I say that Christians should be converted pagans, therefore, I am certainly not referring to anything in the eclectic mixture of Wiccan or neo-pagan practice that, as Hutton says, is a faith "set in a 'prehistoric fairyland.'"[9] But neither am I simply dismissing neo-paganism as one more example of humanity's age-old propensity to idolatry. Such dismissal is the most common Christian reaction to neo-paganism.

Paganism and Karl Barth

Orthodox theologians and biblical scholars have been quick to point out the fatal errors of paganism when it shows up in liberal or feminist theology. A number of books have appeared recently in the evangelical press that warn of the dangers of paganism. Some of these border on the hysterical and partake more than a little of the attitude that, in another era, led people to burn pagans at the stake for witchcraft. But even more careful scholarship condemns paganism, in that it regards the basic pagan premise—that something of "the divine," however conceived, can be seen in nature—as wholly detrimental to salvation in Christ.

Most Protestant thinkers regard any attempt to see a response to creation as a preparation for the Christian gospel as semi-Pelagian

7. Ibid., 22.
8. Ibid., 22.
9. Hutton, *Pagan Religions,* 339.

heresy. Here the classic treatment is the exchange between Karl Barth and Emil Brunner in 1934 that was published in English in 1946 as *Natural Theology*. Brunner attempts to make room, drawing largely on John Calvin, for some kind of "natural theology," some knowledge of God that allows for a point of contact with the unbeliever. His argument is summed up well in these words:

> Wherever God does anything, he leaves the imprint of his nature upon what he does. Therefore the creation of the world is at the same time a revelation, a self-communication of God. This statement is not pagan, but fundamentally Christian.[10]

Brunner goes on to argue that some sort of natural theology based on this imprint of God on creation is "of decisive importance for the dealings of Christians with unbelievers."[11] He attempts to distance himself from various errors, including what he calls the Catholic error of attempting to prove the existence of God. But, he says, "The fact that there is a false apologetic way of making contact does not mean that there is not a right way. . . . Though proof is excluded, this does not exclude the possibility of a discussion pointing towards such evidence of the existence of God as we have."[12]

To all of this, Barth says, "Nein!" (the title of the pamphlet that contains his response). It is only the witness of the Spirit that allows people to know God. Knowledge of God is always God's work; it is not anything that humans achieve. Human "knowledge" of God through creation is always, he says, twisted into idolatrous paganism. Thus, the only way in which we can possibly read and understand Romans 1:20, which speaks of the knowledge of God through "what has been made," is that it seals our human culpability in turning not to God but to idols of our own making.

It is difficult to understand the passion of this exchange apart from its setting in the Germany of the 1930s, where the theological liberalism rooted in two centuries of Enlightenment confidence in

10. *Natural Theology, Comprising "Nature and Grace" by Professor Dr. Emil Brunner and the Reply "No!" by Dr. Karl Barth,* trans. Peter Fraenkel (London: Geoffrey Bles, 1946), 25.

11. Ibid., 55.

12. Ibid.

human reason was being transmuted all too easily into a "German Christianity," which was comfortable with Hitler's doctrines of blood and soil. Even given that context, however, it is difficult to see how Barth's effective exclusion of any trace of God from creation is consistent with Scripture, which makes it plain that "the heavens declare the glory of God; the skies proclaim the work of his hands" (Ps. 19:1). Such an exclusion, it seems to me, seeks to protect the holiness of the Creator by effectively ignoring the creation's witness to God. In so doing, it contributes to the ultimately Gnostic idea that salvation in Christ has nothing to do with the changeable and imperfect reality of our creatureliness.

Paganism and Feminism

Christian scholars have often found the rapid growth of radical feminism another good reason to say "Nein" to any attempt to see neo-paganism as the sign of more than idolatrous error. The close connection between some feminism and paganism appears in the apparently innocent attempt to use the occasional feminine imagery for God in Scripture as a basis for speaking of God mainly in feminine terms. In the prayers and liturgies of some ostensibly Christian denominations, it is now simply unacceptable to speak of God as "Father." The preferred terms are either neutral ("divine parent"), inclusive ("Father and Mother"), or simply feminine ("Mother") in a kind of affirmative action that, at best, seeks to correct several millennia of what is perceived as patriarchal error by way of a period of matriarchal compensation.

Perhaps the most notorious instance of such an attempt to bring Christianity and goddess worship together was the "Re-imaging God" conference in 1994. Women from many American Protestant denominations gathered with the purpose of expunging all hints of patriarchy from Christian worship and expression. An often-cited liturgy from that conference, in worship of Sophia (widely asserted to be a feminine face of God), underlines how total such a "reimaging" can be—and how cut off it is from Scripture:

> Our maker Sophia, we are women in your image: With the hot blood of our wombs we give form to new life. With the courage of our convictions we pour out lifeblood for justice. Sophia, creator

God, let your milk and honey flow. . . . Our sweet Sophia, we are
women in your image: with nectar between our thighs we invite
a lover, we birth a child with our warm body fluids, we remind the
world of its pleasures and sensations. . . . Our guide, Sophia, we
are women in your image: with our moist mouths we kiss away a
tear, we smile encouragement. With the honey of wisdom in our
mouths, we prophesy a full humanity to all the peoples.[13]

Christian scholars have been quick to point out the essentially
pagan nature of such prayers and the attempt to make feminine
experience of natural cycles, which women clearly embody in a
much more profound way than men, the basis of a new way of
talking about God.

The thought of Elizabeth Achtemeier is particularly helpful
here in pointing out the way in which Christians should *not* be pagans. In an article called "Exchanging God for 'No Gods': A Discussion of Female Language for God," she writes in defense of the in-
escapable fact that the God of the Bible, whom all agree is not a
gendered being, is nevertheless revealed in masculine language:

The basic reason for that designation of God is that the God of the
Bible will not let himself be identified with his creation, and therefore human beings are to worship not the creation but the Creator.
. . . To be sure, God works in his creation through the instruments
of his Word and Spirit; he orders his creation and sustains it; he
constantly cares for it; but he is never identified with it. And it is
that holiness, that otherness, that transcendence of the Creator,
which also distinguishes Biblical religion from all others.[14]

The problem with feminine language for God, as Achtemeier
and many others have pointed out, is that it makes it fatally easy
to conflate Creator with creation, making the transcendent Creator into the immanent "Mother Nature," she who gives birth. If
(as many feminist liturgies today suggest) creation issues from the
"womb of God," then it is made of the same stuff as God, and we
ourselves are made of God-stuff. It is not far from such a view of
God to various pagan attempts to reenact divine creativity by

13. Cited in Carl E. Braaten and Robert W. Jenson, eds., *Either/Or: The Gospel or Neo-Paganism* (Grand Rapids: Eerdmans, 1995), 3.
14. In *Speaking the Christian God: The Holy Trinity and the Challenge of Feminism,* ed. Alvin F. Kimel, Jr. (Grand Rapids: Eerdmans, 1992), 8.

means of our own activity, including sexual activity. Thus, Achtemeier eloquently concludes:

> The feminists, believing themselves divine, think that by their own power they can restructure society, restore creation, and overcome suffering. But the tortured history of humankind testifies to what human beings do when they think they are a law unto themselves with no responsibility to God, and those feminists who are claiming that God is in them will equally fall victim to human sin.[15]

Salvation is not something we can accomplish ourselves: For it we need a God who is "wholly other," who acts quite apart from any of our own efforts to please him. Achtemeier echoes the great truths discovered and rediscovered by Calvin and Barth. Because paganism is so prone to move from glimpsing God in nature to trying to *imitate* God in nature, and thus ignoring the only power that can save us, that of the transcendent God, these Christian scholars are adamantly against any trace of seeing God in nature, which they rightly dismiss as pagan.

Paganism and Paul

In the face of both the discouraging evidence concerning those who call themselves pagans today and the strong and eloquent words of scholars such as Barth and Achtemeier, let me now return to the basic thesis of this paper, which is that Christian salvation is ideally a converted rather than a rejected paganism. To make that case, it is necessary to look more closely at the origins of the word *pagan*—and to look at the way the Christian gospel of salvation first came to the pagan world in the preaching of Paul.

Pagan literally means "dweller in the country." Its original meaning was something like "rural" as opposed to "urban." In fact, originally *pagan* bore the same relationship to *paganus*, "countryside," as the word *urban* bears to *urbus*, "city."

The reasons for the shift of meaning from "rural" to "anti-Christian" are not difficult to find. For good strategic reasons, Christianity spread largely in urban centers, partly, of course, because that is

15. Ibid., 16.

where the people were concentrated. Antioch, Corinth, Athens, and Rome were centers of culture and commerce, and it made sense to concentrate on these locations. Also, the first Christian missionaries followed a pattern of going to the Jewish synagogue in an area and arguing that Jesus was the Messiah whom the Hebrew Scriptures promised. Already the Jews of the diaspora were a largely urban people; Paul did not visit synagogues in rural areas. As a result, Christianity grew first mainly among urban populations. Thus, the old religions maintained their vitality longer in the countryside. For the sophisticated urban dweller, "pagan" already had the connotation of "bumpkin" or "hick." To that already derogatory connotation was gradually added the meaning "unbeliever" or "idolater" as the cities (particularly after the conversion of Constantine) became more and more Christian. (A similar history lies behind the word *heathen,* which orginally meant "dweller in the heath.")

Country people were, for a variety of reasons, slower to change their ways than dwellers in the city, many of whom were (as now) uprooted from their own particular *paganus* to begin with. Even today Christianity grows most rapidly among displaced peoples—thus, refugee camps and immigrant communities are often fertile soil for evangelism. But is it good to be a placeless Christian? Does becoming part of the body of Christ necessarily involve ceasing to be a part of the body of the earth and those various seasonal and vegetative cycles that paganism celebrates?

How does one present the gospel of salvation in Christ to those who are rooted in a place—to pagans, in this original sense? Here the model of Paul is instructive. His method of evangelization involved rooting the gospel in the revelation that the people already had. Thus, when he spoke to the Jews, he spoke of God's covenant with Abraham, his mighty acts toward that covenant people, and the promise of a Messiah. Only then did he speak of Jesus as that Messiah. In none of his sermons to Jewish audiences did Paul speak of creation—not, of course, because the Jews did not believe in creation, but rather because they had received a more complete word from God in the law and the prophets and understood creation within the framework of that revelation.

In the two cases in which Luke reported Paul's sermon to pagans, Paul again rooted the message of salvation in what the people already knew of God. In both these cases he began not with God's word in history and Scripture but with God's inarticulate word in creation. It is, in a sense, the original state of humanity to be pagan—that is, to dwell in the country, enmeshed in and inseparable from the webs and cycles of creation. People thus dependent on creation are able to acknowledge it as a gift; this is what Paul in Romans 1 referred to as "what may be known about God" by all people (v. 19). That knowledge, in its incompleteness, becomes the context for the fuller word from God in Jesus. It too appeals to a covenant—but to one older than the one made with Abraham. The reaffirmation of the Creator's goodness forms the covenant made by God with Noah and (significantly) with *every creature* that was with him in the ark. The substance of this covenant affirms the cycles of creation, as do the pagans, but the covenant roots these cycles firmly in the gift of the transcendent God: "As long as the earth endures, seedtime and harvest, cold and heat, summer and winter, day and night will never cease" (Gen. 8:22). It is in this universal covenant that Paul rooted his preaching to the pagans.

The best example of this method involves the pagans in Lystra, in the mountainous interior of Turkey. The story is told in Acts 14. When Paul and Barnabas healed a man lame from birth, the people—with extraordinary enthusiasm—identified them immediately as the gods Hermes and Zeus and sought to make them the object of pagan worship, complete with wreaths and bulls. The story is particularly interesting because it almost certainly reflects the belief in a local legend told in Ovid's *Metamorphoses*. An old, impoverished couple, Glaucus and Philemon, welcome to their meager table two travelers who have been denied hospitality by every household in the wealthy valley below. As they eat their meal, the wine jar keeps flowing with the finest wine, and the couple recognize that their guests are Zeus and Hermes in human form. They are rewarded by having their hut changed to a palace—and the inhospitable valley below is wiped out by a flood. With this story as a background, the Lystrans' enthusiastic welcome is understandable. But Paul was quick to identify himself as an ordinary man and to beg them to turn from the "worthless things" of pagan worship. At the same time, his reply is significant because it implicitly acknowledged that in their mistaken worship they were reflecting a knowledge of:

> the living God, who made heaven and earth and sea and every-thing in them. In the past, he let all nations go their own way. Yet he has not left himself without testimony: He has shown kindness by giving you rain from heaven and crops in their seasons; he provides you with plenty of food and fills your hearts with joy.
>
> Acts 14:15–17

Paul was quick both to distance the gospel of salvation from pagan practice and to connect it with pagan belief—the belief that the regularities of creation that fill their bodies with food and their hearts with joy are indeed a gift, however mysterious and prone to misunderstanding. As John Stott puts it in commenting on this passage, "With the pagans in Lystra he focused not on a Scripture which they did not know, but on the natural world around them, which they did know and could see." Stott continues (in implicit disagreement with Barth):

> We have to begin where people are, to find a point of contact with them. With secularized people today this might be what constitutes authentic humanness, the universal quest for tran-scendence, the hunger for love and community, the search for freedom, or the longing for personal significance.[16]

Stott is clear, however (and here he is in agreement with Barth), that "wherever we begin . . . we shall end with Jesus Christ, who is himself the good news, and who alone can fulfill all human aspirations."[17]

Paul followed the same pattern when he spoke to the more philosophically sophisticated pagans (they should more accu-rately be called urbans, though their roots were in the *paganus*) in Athens. His approach was to connect explicitly the "un-known God" of their worship with the living God. Once again Paul had no room for pagan practice or worship itself. As Stott observes, Paul was praising the admission of their ignorance

16. *The Spirit, the Church, and the World* (Downers Grove, Ill.: InterVarsity, 1990), 232.
17. Ibid.

(that the true God was unknown) rather than the various errors of their excessive religiosity.[18] But the fact that their pagan worship was rooted in some sense of the reality of the true God, however unknown, was unavoidable. Once again, Paul connected the knowledge of this God with creation: He "made the world and everything in it" (Acts 17:24). And though God is clearly other than the world (not in any sense "mother" or "womb"), he is "not far from each one of us" (v. 27). Paul even quoted with approval the Stoic poet who speaks of God in a womb-like metaphor: "In him we live and move and have our being" (v. 28).[19] Once again, Paul was ruthless in his criticism of pagan idolatry but surprisingly tolerant—even approving— of the pagan urge to worship.

It is this urge to worship in the face of the gift of creation that we must not quench in dealing with contemporary pagans who, in an increasingly virtual and artificial world, are responding in worship to one of the few things they encounter that is genuine: the gifts of God in creation.

It is often poets who express most clearly the basic pagan knowledge of the first covenant: that creation with its cycles and regularities is a gift. Consider, for example, the work of American Mary Oliver. Her work nowhere suggests she is a Christian, but almost every poem expresses her gratitude for the world as a gift. She begins one poem with the simple statement:

> Every morning
> the world
> is created.[20]

---

18. Ibid., 285.

19. This text is the only clear biblical support for the theological position that has come to be called "panetheism," a term that refers to the belief that "all is in God." Although the term can be defended within the framework of orthodox understanding (as Jurgen Moltman, for example, does in *God in Creation*), the term is used widely to refer to a kind of merging of Creator and creation for which "pantheism" is a better name. (See, for example, the works of Thomas Berry and Matthew Fox and the journal *Creation Spirituality*.) Given these divergences in the way the word is used, it is probably better to avoid it. Properly understood, though, the term can convey something of the reality of the foundational truth expressed most clearly in Colossians 1:17: "In him [Christ] all things hold together."

20. "Morning Poem," in *New and Selected Poems* (Boston: Beacon, 1992), 106.

She proceeds to describe the reappearance of a pond with its flowers and trees out of the darkness. Whether you are by nature happy or sad, she concludes:

> each pond with its blazing lilies
> is a prayer heard and answered
> lavishly,
> every morning,
>
> whether or not
> you have ever dared to be happy,
> whether or not
> you have ever dared to pray.[21]

This suggestion that the proper response to creation is prayer and worship—not of creation itself but of its unknown source—was made in a similar away by another American poet, Denise Levertov, who wrote in a work describing her response to the ordinary but mysterious details of nature:

> this need to dance,
> this need to kneel:
> this mystery:[22]

Both Oliver and Levertov begin with the unexplained sense of happiness—that same sense that Paul connected with the gift of the living God when at Lystra he said that it is he who sends the seasons and "fills your hearts with joy." Of these two poets, it is quite clear that Levertov at least eventually came to know the Person behind the mystery that prompted her to dance and kneel. Quite late in her life she wrote a long poem called "The Mass of St. Thomas Didymus, Skeptic." She says that when she began it she was an agnostic; when she came to its end, she realized she was a Christian, believing that the Creator of all had become flesh in Jesus. Early in the poem she speaks in lines that both praise the beauty of the world and lament its mystery and silence:

21. Ibid.
22. "Of Being," in *The Stream and the Sapphire* (New York: New Directions, 1997), 4.

> Yet our hope lies
> in the unknown,
> in our unknowing.
>
> O deep, remote unknown,
> O deep unknown, Have mercy upon us.

By the end of the poem, however, she finds her prayer answered, first with a possibility that presents itself as a question:

> But can the name
> utter itself
> in the downspin of time?
> Can it enter
> the void?

Then she finds its answer:

> The word
> chose to become
> flesh. In the blur of flesh
> we bow, baffled.[23]

Levertov's progression traces a typical path: from a kind of paganism—grateful for the gift of creation, reverent but agnostic toward its source—to a knowledge that God has restored creation in Christ. This is the basic human experience. We must find ourselves in the mystery of God's gift of creation before we are found by God in the mysterious gift of salvation. Otherwise, we are redeemed ghosts. Another poet, Annie Dillard, put this part of the human condition well at the beginning of her great meditation on creatureliness, *Pilgrim at Tinker Creek:* "We wake, if we ever wake at all, to mystery, rumors of death, beauty, violence. . . . 'Seems like we're just set down here,' a woman said to me recently, 'and don't nobody know why.'"[24]

Perhaps it is this same sense of divine mystery in creation that the writer of Ecclesiastes speaks of when he says, "I have seen the burden God has laid on men. He has made everything beautiful in its time. He has also set eternity in the hearts of men; yet they cannot fathom what God has done from beginning to end" (3:10–11).

23. In *Poems 1972–1982* (New York: New Directions, 2001), 266, 273.
24. (New York: Harper & Row, 1974), 2.

When I say that Christians should be redeemed pagans, I mean that salvation is a transformation and restoration of our creature-liness. This transformation of the incarnate *creatureliness* of the Creator in Christ is central. No one has put this connection be-tween creation and salvation better than Athanasius:

> The first fact that you must grasp is this: *the renewal of creation has been wrought by the Self-same Word Who made it in the be-ginning.* There is thus no inconsistency between creation and salvation; for the One Father has employed the same Agent for both works, effecting the salvation of the world through the same Word Who made it at the first.[25]

The fact that creation, because of our sinful, broken, and in-complete involvement with it, requires our salvation is common-place in Christian thought. But the reverse is not as obvious: that salvation is for the whole creation as well. It is our creatureliness that is restored in Christ. The pagan attempt to restore harmony with the divinity glimpsed in creation through various ritual at-tempts to be one with the cycles of nature is (as Paul pointed out at Lystra and Athens) a dangerous and idolatrous vanity. But it is just as dangerous to understand salvation in a way that cuts us off from our creatureliness. And this has been the tendency in much Christian understanding of salvation. There are reasons beyond simple human sinfulness that make the spiritually hungry people of our time turn away from Christianity. One is that they often see a Christianity that understands salvation as deliverance from a fallen creation rather than the first step in its restoration.

That conviction was expressed to me clearly a few years ago. I received a letter from a pastor in response to a lecture I had given suggesting that salvation in Christ has a creational scope:

> Christ's redemption is always in purchasing the chosen or elect from their trespasses. . . . The redemption of the earth from its groaning will be its vaporization and replacement. Its value is in providing our habitation; it is a variable, we are the constant with God. Praise the Lord that his promise is made so clear to those that want to hear.

25. *On the Incarnation* (Crestwood, N.Y.: St. Vladimir's Orthodox Theolog-ical Seminary, n.d.), 26 (emphasis added).

It is instructive to compare that letter with another recently received from a woman who makes it clear that she is not a Christian. She writes:

> I come from a secular, science, environmental education background. I recently received my masters in teaching and have currently been teaching science in the outdoors to students in grades 5–12. Spending extended periods of time in the wilderness, away from the noise of the city, has made me more aware of the presence of a power bigger than myself. It has brought me closer to the Truth that exists and deepened my relationship with this Truth. I am extremely curious about the ways in which I feel called to live and serve others and have been searching to find fellowship in studying this Truth. Because I was not raised in a religion I have been curious about exploring many different faiths. I currently have been studying the bible and have been blown away by the wisdom I have found in the Gospels.

This attitude of reverent questioning inspired by a truth glimpsed in creation is not, I think, going to be led further by the conviction that creation is nothing more than a backdrop for the human story, destined for "vaporization and replacement." Nor, I suspect, can this woman's sense of truth in creation (and her words are typical of many today) be dismissed with a Barthian "Nein."

Paganism and C. S. Lewis

The extraordinary effectiveness of C. S. Lewis in conveying "mere Christianity" to our time has been endlessly studied. But usually overlooked is the place of paganism in Lewis's apologetic. In *Surprised by Joy,* Lewis describes himself as "a converted pagan living among apostate Christians." An early poem called "A Cliche Came Out of Its Cage" questions a common truism: "You said 'The world is going back to Paganism.' O bright Vision!" He proceeds to define the England of his time in terms recalling the best of Greek paganism:

> I saw . . . Leavis with Lord Russell wreathed in flowers, heralded
>   with flutes
> Leading white bulls to the cathedral of the solemn Muses
> To pay where due the glory of their latest theorem.

And he concludes:

> Heathenism come again, the circumspection and the holy
> fears. . . .
> You said it. Did you mean it? O inordinate liar, stop.[26]

Not that Lewis would be so positive about the eclectic and self-indulgent beliefs of much contemporary self-declared neo-paganism. But he does say, of himself, that he feels he was sent back to the false gods to learn reverence for the time when he would encounter the true God. There is no question—at least by his own testimony—that his is a "post-Christian paganism," which nevertheless found its true object of worship in the Triune God. It is in part those pagan elements that give such power to what is probably the most influential of Lewis's works, the Chronicles of Narnia, in which the entire landscape is peopled by figures from Greek, Celtic, and Norse pagan mythology. (Yet in those stories no reader, young or old, doubts the lordship of the great Lion Aslan.)

But Lewis's most explicit Christian defense of paganism is his allegorical *Pilgrim's Regress*, an early attempt to tell the story of his own conversion. In it the pilgrim John, traveling through "the Landlord's" country on his way to a frankly pagan vision of "an island in the West," encounters a "Grand Canyon" named *Peccatum Adae* (Sin of Adam), which can be crossed only in the company of a rather unattractive old lady called Mother Kirk. John and his companion explore north and south along the canyon. The territory north of the canyon represents all the errors of excessive abstraction and intellectualization—sins of the mind, perhaps. (Interestingly, in his preface, written ten years later, Lewis places Barth among these "northern" errors.) South of the canyon are the errors of excessive feeling: Here belong most of the sins we would consider New Age, occult, and pagan. Yet it is to the south that John is drawn. In his desperate attempt to cross the canyon on his own power by means of a precipitous path down the southern wall of the canyon, he spends a night and a day in a hermit's cave. The hermit is History, and he explains the role of Paganism. The pagans, he says, are those who respond to "pic-

---

26. In *Poems*, ed. Walter Hooper (New York: Harcourt, Brace and World, 1964), 3–4.

tures" sent from the Landlord—myths or stories that never let their desire for him completely die. Sometimes it is a picture of "the gods"; sometimes (as in Romanticism) it is a picture of the land itself. In addition, says History, the Landlord has chosen a particular people, "the shepherd people" (the Jews), to whom he gave "the Rules." Lewis's allegory is extraordinarily rich, too much so to do it justice here. But this outline helps us make sense of a few passages with which I will end this reflection on the role of paganism and Christian salvation.

> Even where Mother Kirk is nominally the ruler men can grow old without knowing how to read the Rules. Her empire is always crumbling. But it never quite crumbles: for as often as men become Pagans again, the Landlord again sends them pictures and stirs up sweet desire and so leads them back to Mother Kirk even as he led the actual Pagans long ago. There is, indeed, no other way.[27]

> In Theology also there is a North and South. The one cries "drive out the bondmaid's son," and the other "Quench not the smoking flax." The one exaggerates the distinctness between Grace and Nature into a sheer opposition and by vilifying the higher levels of Nature (the real *preparatio evangelica* inherent in certain immediately sub-Christian experiences) makes the way hard for those who are at the point of coming in. The other blurs the distinction altogether, flatters mere kindliness into thinking it is charity and vague optimisms or pantheisms into thinking that they are Faith, and makes the way out fatally easy and imperceptible for the budding apostate. The two extremes do not coincide with Romanism (to the North) and Protestantism (to the South). Barth might well have been placed among my Pale Men, and Erasmus might have found himself at home with Mr. Broad.[28]

Not that Lewis has any illusion about the dangers of paganism:

27. C. S. Lewis, *The Pilgrim's Regress* (Grand Rapids: Eerdmans, 1958), 152–53. Significantly, *Pilgrim's Regress* was published in 1933, the same time as the controversy between Brunner and Barth about "natural revelation." In a foreword written for the second edition ten years later, Lewis suggests that Barth might well be placed "north" of the road.

28. Ibid., 12.

The Pagans, because they were under the enemy, were beginning at the wrong end; they were like lazy schoolboys attempting eloquence before they learn grammar. They had pictures for
their eyes instead of roads for their feet, and that is why most of
them could do nothing but desire and then, through starved desire, become corrupt in their imaginations, and so awake and
despair, and so desire again.[29]

Yet despite this danger—and *Surprised by Joy* makes it plain
that he is writing from painful experience—Lewis does not back
off from his conviction that a kind of paganism is basic to our humanity, as basic, in fact, as is our sense of right and wrong (whose
story he tells in the other pilgrim in the allegory, an exceedingly
conscientious and disciplined young man named Vertue). In
speaking of "the people of the Law," Lewis has his hermit History
say, in response to the charge of Jewish narrowness:

They *were* narrow. The thing they had charge of was narrow: it
was the Road. They found it. They sign-posted it. They kept it
clear and repaired it. But you must not think I am setting them
up against the Pagans. The truth is that a Shepherd is only half
a man, and a Pagan is only half a man, so that neither people
was well without the other, nor could either be healed until the
Landlord's Son came into the country.[30]

This necessary "narrowness" is opposed to the breadth of the
kind of revelation that underlies paganism. Lewis calls it "a thing
as widespread and as necessary (though withal as dangerous) as
the sky!"[31]

"Widespread" and "necessary" and at the same time "dangerous." Those are good words to help us discover the ways in which
we are pagans—that is, God-sustained dwellers in the cycles of
God-sustained creation. In this sense, Christians are redeemed pagans, for (to quote one more time from Lewis's allegory) "that is
the definition of a Pagan—a man so travelling that if all goes well
he arrives at Mother Kirk's chair and is carried over this gorge."
That is a good word to our largely pagan times. But we must not

29. Ibid., 154.
30. Ibid., 155.
31. Ibid.

forget the word of caution that Lewis's "History" leaves us with: "The trouble about Pagus [or Vancouver, for example] is that the perfect, and in that sense typical, Pagan is so uncommon there. . . . You see that it is a starting point from which *one* road leads home and a thousand roads lead into the wilderness."[32]

The "perfect Pagan" is one who follows the hints of God's presence in creation to the one place where he can really be known: in Jesus. But many go only deeper into the wilderness (literal and symbolic). The church, sadly, does not often meet them there to point out the "one road that leads home." But that fact should not keep those of us who have some knowledge of the road from directing other pilgrims on to it.

32. Ibid.

Part 3
Responses

8

What's Evangelical about Evangelical Soteriology?

JOHN WEBSTER

What's evangelical about evangelical soteriology? In their different ways, the essays in this volume propose that a soteriology that is authentically evangelical—one that is governed by the gospel of Christ—will, of necessity, have a broader range than has been customary in a good deal of evangelical church life and theology. Though they make the point in different ways—some by exegesis, some by historical analysis, some by a rather more informal mix of Christian teaching and cultural comment—the essays, taken together, are a collective suggestion that "evangelical" soteriology covers a great deal more ground than some dominant strands of contemporary evangelicalism are disposed to believe. And, on that basis, they appeal for a revision of thinking, a reorientation of action, and not a little repentance.

One way of getting hold of the proposals assembled here is to ask, Which aspects of Christian teaching come to the fore? and, correspondingly, Which aspects of Christian teaching are in some measure retracted? Asking these questions is important in grasping the intent of any theological proposal because, in a real sense, all theology is polemical, not in the sense of ill-tempered, bitter, or hostile but in the more basic sense of *occa-sional*. Most theology is written with an eye to its occasioning circumstances—with an eye, that is, to what it identifies as the main theological trends in the constituency it addresses, and with the intention of reinforcing, criticizing, or, perhaps, re-versing those trends. These essays are no exception: They offer a set of judgments about the matters in the Christian gospel to which evangelicals should attend with especial scrupulousness in the light of the evangelical past (recent and more distant) and the main thrust of the gospel's testimony.

Which aspects of Christian teaching come to the fore here? The essays do not represent a school, nor even an agreed on set of positions, but they do betray a number of common points where the authors' theological consciences are exercised, and identifying these points is constructive. One such point to which reference is made in a number of the essays is the insep-arability of salvation from the restoration of the *imago Dei*. Theological teaching about the divine image performs a num-ber of tasks in the collection. It is a central motif in ensuring the co-inherence of creation and redemption; it offers a means of emphasizing that salvation concerns the restoration of human fellowship; it roots a Christian understanding of human nature in language about God's relation to his creation; and it serves to underline that the saving work of God includes within it a moral and cultural imperative. The essays are, again, too varied to identify them with one strand in the history of Christian the-ology. Most of them, however, betray at least some influence from the tradition of "common grace," which has played a sub-stantial role in conservative Protestant theology, ethics, and so-cial-cultural commentary.

Cherith Fee Nordling's essay is particularly instructive in this regard. Here, the *imago Dei* is expounded as relationality—as relative to the Triune God, into whose inner *koinōnia* we are drawn to participate by his saving work, and as relative to other humans, for salvation liberates the sinner for human fellow-ship. In similar fashion, Vincent Bacote appeals to the tie not only between salvation and co-humanity but also between sal-vation and pneumatology, the Spirit being defined as one who imparts "zest for the world." Again, with rather more exegetical orientation, Rikk Watts ties creation and redemption to the image of God, protesting against the apparently attenuated accounts of creation in some soteriologies and proposing an account of salvation as "new creational restoration." Finally, we should note Amy Sherman's deployment of eschatology to give an account of the *telos* of salvation in the city of the redeemed.

The proposals both reinforce and are reinforced by a reading of the situation in which at least North American evangelicalism continues to find itself. Despite the fact that a good deal of evangelical church life and theology have largely disavowed what has been seen as an evangelical overreaction to the immanentist social ethics of liberal Protestantism, a number of the essayists still felt it necessary to press home the point that the social entailments of redemption are not appendages to an otherwise privatized soteriology but ingredients within that which God accomplishes. The North American career of evangelical Protestantism has been deeply shaped by appeals to experience—whether as a foil to formalism, as resistance to intellectualism, or (more worryingly) as a concession to the expressivism of its cultural environment—and these essays join the chorus of protest against the losses sustained in our apprehension of the gospel if such appeals go unchallenged.

Which aspects of Christian teaching are in some measure retracted, or less operative, in the accounts of salvation offered here? We can begin by noting how "salvation" is used in a variety of ways in the course of the essays. Sometimes (as in Henri Blocher's entirely justified critique of the polarizations of Gustaf Aulén's history of soteriology, which is still, *mirabile dictu*, considered a reliable guide to the history of theology) the term coincides with its standard usage in dogmatics to signify the nature and ends of the works of Christ in relation to his person. More often, it is used a good deal more loosely, referring partly to the divine economy of reconciliation, partly to the Son's atoning work, partly to the state of reconciliation between God and humankind to which we are restored, partly to the human future. Such variety, of course, simply reflects biblical and traditional usage. Yet is there not a thicket of problems close to hand here, which many of the essayists do not appear either to have noticed or to have looked at with sufficient alarm? The issue is this: Can the broad reference of "salvation" be sustained without in some measure drawing attention away from the utterly unique and gratuitous character of God's saving work, willed by the Father, effected by the Son's obedience to the Father's will, and realized both now and in the future by the promise of the Holy Spirit?

With the exception, once again, of Blocher, none of the authors offers a sustained exposition of the dogmatics of salvation, nor of the biblical testimony that dogmatics serves. Themes such as justification, sacrifice, and ransom; Christ as prophet, priest, and king; and the Spirit as the bearer of Christ's saving benefits either do not appear or have only walk-on parts. This may be because such material is assumed, leaving the authors free to explore the ramifications of salvation for human common life. Yet one might at least ask whether— given the massive presence of an immanentist moral and political culture—they can afford *not* to invest in giving a depiction of the dogmatics that has to underlie soteriology as moral theory. One of the most crucial reasons for undertaking such a portrayal is to secure the point that whatever is said *rightly* about salvation in human social and moral space can be said only on the basis of the divine initiative, an initiative that is not just the first impulse in a train of actions undertaken by the church or humankind but sovereign at every point in the economy of salvation. What is at issue, in other words, is the reference of salvation to the divine grace. One of the chief reasons for the church to get its theological mind around the great clumsy conceptual vocabulary of patristic Christology and of later soteriology is to offer a blockage against moralism, for the language of substance, persons, and natures; of missions; and of justification, merit, and substitution offers an ontology of the work of God that, far from being abstractly unconnected to the life of society and politics, instructs us in the divine action that alone makes human fellowship possible and necessary.

None of this is a denial of what many of the essays seek to affirm—namely, that there is (in Bruce Hindmarsh's nice word) a "spaciousness" to salvation without which we cannot do justice to the work of God for us. It is more an invitation to reflect on the sheerly objective, given character of God's work *extra nos,* which alone is the condition of God's work *pro nobis* and *in nobis* and of our works of fellowship. And it is also a suggestion that the legitimate concerns articulated by a number of the essays might profitably be clarified by a trinitarian moral ontology. That is, what is required is an account of the way the world *is* because it is the theater of God's merciful work of reconciliation, and so of the way in which righteous action is truthful. We do well to remember that it was, after all, just such a lack of moral and dogmatic ontology that proved so ruinous in the nineteenth-century liberal tradition and its twentieth-century heirs.

A final comment concerns method. Some papers fall more recognizably within the acknowledged theological sub-disciplines—Hindmarsh's elegant and scrupulous historical account, Blocher's historical-dogmatic analysis, Watts's historical-exegetical study. Others are more eclectic, assembling a case by appealing to cultural theory, some exegesis (biblical and doctrinal), and a good deal of informal observations of church life and its contexts. Am I alone in worrying whether some more sharply focused judgment about the norms and sources of theology would be helpful here?

One of the essayists—Loren Wilkinson—is more direct in setting out an account of the kind of theology that is being undertaken: a correlationist apologetic underpinned by a theology of common grace (Kuyper would be happy; Bavinck would, I think, be a bit troubled). Whether neo-paganism is a *praeparatio evangelii* I doubt very much; nor am I disposed to interpret Romans 1 and Acts 17 as indicators of common grace; nor would I begin my exegetical reflections on paganism there: I would start with the Apocalypse. But the most pressing issue raised here is the price that theology has to pay for its engagement in apologetics. Wilkinson is right that what Barth discerned in Brunner's eristics (and might have found in C. S. Lewis's bluff attempts to persuade the educated worldling) was a set of instincts shared by the German Christians. At the very least, that ought to make us pause.

Whatever be made of that issue (I do not pretend to carry that day), these essays ought to set the agenda for an evangelical theological debate about salvation. Will it resist the drift into the private, the isolation of the affections from reason and common life? Will it honor its history as a whole, which has had more than expressivist strands? Above all, will it engage with the gospel of God's covenant-restoring mercy of which the Son's person and mission are the enactment and of which the Spirit is the communicative presence? We shall see.

9

Clarifying Vision, Empowering Witness

JONATHAN R. WILSON

The essays collected in this volume are meant to represent an expansion of the horizons of the evangelical doctrine of salvation. That assignment, of course, presumes some vision of the present horizons. Although the task of identifying evangelical horizons is not undertaken in this volume, these essays nevertheless come together as an effective expansion of evangelical vision.

One intriguing exercise that I commend to readers is inferring from these essays what the present horizons of salvation actually are in evangelicalism. Another worthy exercise is discerning the multiple audiences of the essays. My main concern, however, is discussing the following: three themes that seem to recur throughout the collection and represent the main lines of a necessary broadening of evangelical soteriology; two doctrines that should have been more significant in the collection; and one issue that takes us beyond this collection into a broader discussion in which evangelicals must engage as we seek to be more faithful to Scripture and our mission.

Three Themes

One of the significant contributions in this collection is what I will call salvation as *teleological.* By this I mean the exposition of salvation as a goal-directed process. This teleology is evident in most of the essays. As Amy Sherman notes, evangelicals have long been good at describing "salvation *from*" but not so good at describing "salvation *for.*" This *for* identifies the *telos* (plural *telē*) of salvation. The rich variety of the *telē* identified in the collection reflects the rich variety of Scripture. Sherman points to the heavenly city; Cherith Fee Nordling imagines the renewed *imago Dei;* Rikk Watts announces the new exodus/new creation; Vincent Bacote turns us to the *telos* of salvation in this life.

Each of these *telē* is developed in faithfulness to the biblical teaching. What is not so clear is the relationship among them. In the list, we find future and present, social (city), natural (new creation), historical (new exodus), and personal (Nordling's *imago Dei*). Perhaps what this richness reveals is the incomprehensible depth and breadth of the salvation that is accomplished in Jesus Christ. This is a great service to evangelical theology, which has long obscured these riches by overemphasizing "salvation from" soteriology.

The overall teleological thrust of the essays adds another dimension to evangelical soteriology. If we learn to think with Scripture of a teleological soteriology, then we must also think of salvation as a process. This raises some tensions for an evangelicalism among whose distinctives is "conversionism." Here we need continued work on a conversionist spirituality and a soteriology of discipleship. Evangelicals have promoted spirituality and discipleship in various ways, but in most varieties of evangelicalism, those promotions have been "value added" to salvation, not an intrinsic part of salvation. Now that we have some good accounts of a teleological soteriology, let some of us move on to a more robust teleological account of conversion and a soteriology of discipleship.[1]

Before we leave teleology behind, I must note a missing element. I do not know how intentionally teleological the various es-

1. A good start on this is Gordon T. Smith, *Beginning Well: Christian Conversion and Authentic Transformation* (Downers Grove, Ill.: InterVarsity, 2001).

sayists were. But even if they were simply adopting and responding to the images of Scripture that are unavoidably teleological, one image is striking by its absence: the image of final judgment and wrath. Here we have to move carefully, because judgment is not obviously part of the teleology of salvation. In much theology, condemnation seems to inscribe another *telos* alongside, even in conflict with, salvation. We tend to think of salvation and condemnation as different, sometimes opposed, works of God. Yet precisely here we could think insightfully about the place of wrath and condemnation in a teleological soteriology.

In such an account (which I cannot give here), condemnation is part of the teleology of salvation. That is, God must judge things according to their relation to God. All that is evil must be judged to be so—as a necessary (teleological) part of God's work of salvation. What enters into the new heaven and new earth? And what is excluded? God's salvation takes place only as God judges. Such a teleological placing of God's wrath would recover one of the contributions of traditional evangelical soteriology. At the same time, it seems to me, such placing would allow the biblical teaching to open up new insights into God's salvation.

In addition to a teleological soteriology, these essays also contain a *cosmological* soteriology. "Cosmological" can mean many things today, but in this case it refers to the salvation of the whole of creation, a theme already noted in the teleological character of these essays.

This cosmological soteriology corrects a tendency in evangelical soteriology and expands our understanding. In some evangelical soteriology (but not restricted to evangelical varieties), salvation becomes, almost by default, docetic. That is, salvation is the salvation of believers *from* creation rather than *with* creation. Several of the essayists (Watts, Nordling, Loren Wilkinson) directly challenge this heretical tendency and help us recover a neglected and essential part of the biblical declaration of salvation in Jesus Christ. They also demonstrate (particularly Wilkinson) the importance of such a recovery for maintaining our balance (not blown about by every wind of doctrine) in the cultural currents of the New Age.

This cosmological recovery also expands our understanding of the scope and intent of salvation beyond a narrow concern for humankind. Some soteriology, though not precisely docetic in its tendency, is nevertheless unbiblically anthropocentric. Certainly, the Good News of salvation in Jesus Christ is good news for humankind, but it is good news for humankind within the redemption of creation. Watts's and Nordling's emphasis on the *imago* grounds this cosmological soteriology in Scripture: Salvation is the redemption of creation, beginning with the salvation of those who are both creatures and God's viceregents over creation. If creation is to be saved, that salvation must begin with the salvation of those meant to care for and rule over creation in God's name.[2]

Although this cosmological soteriology is a welcome correction to and expansion of some evangelical soteriology, I miss among the essays a full integration of the emphasis with evangelical soteriology. To what extent is this cosmological soteriology congruent with traditional evangelical accounts of salvation? Are we being asked to move from an anthropocentric soteriology to a cosmocentric soteriology? Is this emphasis on creation an addition to or a replacement for traditional evangelical soteriology? These essays rightly point us toward lacunae in our soteriology, but we still have work to do to fit it all together in a way that will keep us from simply swinging from one overemphasis to another. As Bruce Hindmarsh's history and Henri Blocher's doctrine remind us, there is much to conserve in the evangelical tradition. The introduction of cosmological soteriology does not deny that, but we need to develop it further to keep the pendulum from swinging too far to the opposite side.

Finally, in relation to this cosmological soteriology, we need a further account of the redemption of creation that makes sense of our experience of "the natural" today in light of our proper claims about its end. How can we affirm the ultimate redemption of creation, at work even now, in the midst of our bodies wasting away, in the midst of epidemics and famines, in the midst of the explanatory power of neo-Darwinism? Certainly, these essays are doing good work as they recover from

2. See my more detailed discussion of this complex issue in Jonathan R. Wilson, "Evangelicals and the Environment: A Theological Concern," *Christian Scholar's Review* 28, no. 2 (winter 1998): 298–307.

Scripture a cosmological soteriology. And certainly, we need to correct our denigration of creation and expand our doctrine of salvation beyond a narrow anthropocentrism. But in our enthusiasm for this recovery, correction, and expansion, we must not race past the hard work incumbent upon us.

Just as many of our contemporaries are discovering a new romanticism in New Age thought, others are discovering a new modernism in neo-Darwinian thought. Thus, a cosmological soteriology must be two-pronged in its development. My intuition is that such an approach will be cruciform and crucicentric, because it is in the cross that we see both the travail of creation (an account superior to neo-Darwinism) and the redemption of creation (an account superior to New Age). Therefore, although the essays in this collection rightly describe a cosmological soteriology, they leave us with more work to do.

The third theme that runs through these essays as an appropriate expansion of evangelical soteriology is *embodiment.* The preacher in me wants to label this strand "physical" soteriology as a companion of teleological and cosmological soteriology, but such a label could be extremely misleading apart from the following exposition.

In my exposition of the cosmological soteriology in these essays, we have already encountered the recovery of cosmos as redeemed creation. In this third strand, we encounter the creatureliness of human beings in our embodiment. This theme gets worked out most fully in Bacote's essay. There embodiment places us in a social and cultural context within which and through which our salvation is worked out. In a similar way, Hindmarsh attends to historical "place" as a sign of our embodiment.

This sense of place significantly expands much recent evangelical soteriology. Hindmarsh and Bacote (other essayists may be implicated here, but I will focus on these two) effectively subvert the disembodied, decontextualized soteriology that has often characterized evangelicalism's tacit accommodation to modernism. In such cases, the dehistoricized, disembodied self is saved without reference to our bodies or the relationships with which our bodies connect us.

Hindmarsh demonstrates that here, more than with the previous two themes, our evangelical heritage provides neglected and

forgotten resources for recovering a richer, more biblical soteriology. Earlier evangelicals were concerned about the place and
particularity of those whom God would save. Hindmarsh's essay
carefully retrieves the cultural moment in which evangelicals advanced a soteriology of personal faith, a "religion of the heart,"
that corrected the civil and ritualistic practice of Christianity.
Perhaps the clue to the fading of this concern for particularity
may be found in Hindmarsh's astute observation that "evangelicalism emerged precisely on the trailing edge of Christendom
and the leading edge of modernity."

If Hindmarsh points us toward historical resources for recovering an embodied soteriology, Bacote systematically calls
us to a contemporary repentance—a changing of our minds
and practices—in soteriology. At first glance, his account of salvation for *this life* may seem at odds with the teleological theme
I earlier identified, but that is not the case. Bacote rightly protests an evangelical soteriology that disembodies salvation.
Such soteriology makes two mistakes. It misconstrues the biblical *telos* of salvation, and it disconnects this present life from
the reality of salvation. Both mistakes must be corrected for
evangelical soteriology to be more faithful to Scripture. The teleological, cosmological, and embodied soteriology of these essays does much to correct that mistake.

Among the four categories articulated by Bacote for a soteriology that focuses on this life, the pneumatological deserves
special emphasis. It seems to me that this is the theological
grounding for an embodied soteriology. The great danger we
face as we expand evangelical soteriology is that our discourse
will be taken over by the cultural moment. Theological grounding, therefore, is crucial. In the case of embodiment, the Spirit
is the one who indwells us, whose sanctifying work in the economy of salvation is particular, and whose gifting for service in
the economy of salvation is individual. And yet, it is the one
Spirit of God, the Spirit of the Messiah.

Two Doctrines

My reference to the Spirit leads directly into the two doctrines that seem to be intrinsic to the essays in this collection

but largely absent from them in any thematized, focused way. My claim here is not that some things were left out. Any project has limitations; I am impressed and instructed by what this collection addresses. But I also want to claim that the concerns represented in these essays call for greater attention to the doctrines of the church and the Trinity.

Although there are some significant gestures toward the church—in Bacote's essay, for example—the church seems to be largely invisible just when it should be coming into view. And even when it comes into view, it seems to fade away quickly again. Perhaps that is the problem: In evangelical theology, the doctrine of the church turns on the invisibility of the true church.[3]

If we are to sustain the expanded biblical soteriology recommended by this volume, we must overcome the near invisibility of the doctrine of the church in evangelicalism, especially its North American variety. Teleological soteriology cannot be sustained apart from a tradition, a community, and its practices. Similarly, a cosmological soteriology asks us to make sense of the claim that all creation is being renewed. Where do we see that if not in the people of God called out to that new life? And our embodied life, the life of the Spirit in us, is precisely the life of that new community, the church.

Sherman calls us to live today toward the new city, and Bacote reminds us that salvation *now* is political. As evangelicals begin to recover the political dimension of salvation, we run the very great risk of simply mirroring the politics of this age. This double play on *polis* (Gk. for "city") in Sherman and Bacote calls for greater evangelical attention to the biblical image of the church as "another city," so that we are able to resist the politics of this age as a means of salvation. At the same time, such an acknowledgment of biblical imagery should remind us that the church is also *oikos*, God's household. The public nature *(polis)* of salvation is balanced by the family nature *(oikos)* of salvation. The church is God's city and God's household. We cannot sustain the expanded soteriology represented in these

3. For some help along these lines, see the essay by Telford Work, "Reordering Salvation: Church as the Proper Context for the *Ordo Salutis*," in *Ecumenical Theology in Worship, Doctrine, and Life: Essays in Honor of Geoffrey Wainwright*, ed. David Cunningham, Ralph Del Colle, and Lucas Lamadrid (New York and Oxford: Oxford University Press, 1999), 182–95.

essays apart from a more robust ecclesiology and, more importantly, the very life of the church itself. In the midst of a movement often marked by "parachurch" life, evangelical theologians must be constantly on guard against that habitual neglect.

I began this section by noting the near invisibility of the doctrine of the church in evangelicalism, especially its North American variety. But that's not quite accurate. What we really have is an implicit, uncriticized doctrine of the church smuggled into our life through marketing strategies, programs, and practices. Our ecclesiology in these instances is utilitarian. What we need as a correction is a biblical, teleological doctrine of the church that is profoundly different from our current doctrine.

The second theme that needs to be incorporated into these accounts is a more explicit trinitarian grammar. None of these essays goes wrong in trinitarian doctrine, but none really makes that grammar basic to its argument. In work of this nature, as scholars seek to break new ground within a particular theological tradition and expand the horizons, the trinitarian shape of our faith needs to be explicit and exposed. That is, it needs to be clear for all to see. Readers need to have the trinitarian economy of the proposals laid bare.

By conforming to this expectation, scholars accomplish two tasks. First, they make themselves accountable to the theological tradition. Only if one can spell out the trinitarian shape of a proposal is it worthy of being called "Christian." Second, scholars give guidance to future work that seeks to continue along the same lines. Without some explicit trinitarian shaping, future workers in these fields may go astray.

Some examples are in order. If our teleological soteriology is not trinitarian, we may fall into one or more errors. If we neglect God the Father, we may not recognize that our end is reconciliation to and praise of the One who is also our beginning. Apart from the recognition of the self-offering of the Son, we may see the end of salvation as the result of negotiations between God the Father and God the Son. Apart from the work of the Holy Spirit, we may regard the *telos* of salvation as a goal for us to achieve rather than a gift to receive.

If our cosmological soteriology is not trinitarian, we will not be able to hold together redemption and creation—the redemption of creation as God's saving work. Redemption and creation hold together in the one "agent" by which they are accomplished in threefold action. Thus, we cannot give an account of cosmological soteriology without also at some level having an account of the one God—Father, Son, and Holy Spirit—acting in creation and redemption.

Finally, as already noted, an embodied soteriology needs a pneumatology, but that pneumatology could quickly stray into the hyper-spirituality of the biblical Corinthians if it is not grounded in Christ crucified. Such trinitarian grammar protects an embodied soteriology from an over-realized eschatology and an overemphasized theology of glory. Yes, our salvation is embodied, but it is embodied in people who are living toward death . . . and then resurrection by the power of the Spirit of him who raised Jesus from the dead.

One Issue

Finally, I suggest for further consideration one issue absent from this volume though very much present in Christian scholarship: the (re)interpretation of the Pauline and Reformation doctrine of justification by faith. I do not fault this volume for its neglect of this debate, for no one volume can do everything. The topics represented here are wisely selected, and I have already noted their considerable importance and excellence.

Nevertheless, over the next several years, evangelicals must devote some attention to justification by faith. That attention is demanded by various factors. Within evangelicalism, the issues arise from the statement "Evangelicals and Catholics Together," the ensuing controversy, and the further statements on "The Gift of Salvation" and "The Gospel: An Evangelical Celebration." In the larger world of Christian scholarship, the meaning of justification by faith has been reopened by a host of scholars: E. P. Sanders, J. D. G. Dunn, Richard Hays, and J. Louis Martyn among them. These New Testament scholars have in various ways proposed different understandings of justification by faith. Sanders's covenantal nomism and Dunn's "new perspective" call into question any sharp distinction between works and faith. Hays and Martyn, with their arguments for "faith" as "the faithfulness of Christ" rather than "faith in Christ," also challenge traditional understandings of justification by faith. In historical theology, some Finnish Luther scholars have offered an alternative context for Luther that connects him more closely with an Orthodox doctrine of salvation.

Since evangelicalism is significantly rooted in the Protestant Reformation (the extent is a matter of controversy), evangelicals must energetically engage these developments. If, following Alasdair MacIntyre, a tradition is a "socially embodied argument" unified in large part by agreement on what is worth arguing about, then surely evangelical theology is a tradition that considers justification by faith worth an argument or two. Evangelical New Testament scholars are making contributions, but there is still work to be done.

The essayists represented in this volume demonstrate admirably the social embodiment of argument about something that matters most—the Good News of God's saving work in Jesus Christ witnessed in the life of the church by the power of the Spirit. Their work expands our vision, calls God's people to an ever renewing way of life, and proclaims God's saving work to our lost world. May we learn from them.

Subject Index

Abelard, Peter, 107
Abraham, 149–50
Achtemeier, Elizabeth, 162–63
Adler, Margot, 155–56, 156 n. 2
Allen, Charlotte, 158–59
Althaus, Paul, 73–74, 89
Ambrose, 75
Anselm, 73, 104 n. 7
antinomianism, 73–74
apologetics, 159–75
Aquinas, Thomas, 130, 130 n. 20
Aristotle, 80, 130 n. 20
Arnold, Clinton, 79
Athanasius, 76, 132 n. 23, 170
atonement
    as *Agnus Victor* paradox, 89–91
    as *Christus Victor*, 69–78
    Martin Luther's conceptions of,
        76–77, 89
    moral influence account of, 107–9
    patristic conceptions of, 74–76
    as penal substitution, 74–75, 77–
        78, 84, 86–89
Augsburg Confession, 77
Augustine, 75, 75 n. 21, 130
Aulén, Gustaf, 67–69, 69 n. 6, 70
        n. 10, 73–78, 74–75 n. 21,
        83, 181
Austin, Margaret, 57

Bacon, Francis, 39
Bacote, Vincent, 180–81, 186, 189,
        190, 191

Barth, Karl, 72, 72 n. 15, 121, 159–61,
        163, 172, 173, 173 n. 27,
        183
Bebbington, David, 47
Beckerleg, Katherine, 19–20
Bible, 16, 18, 80 n. 37, 84, 109, 141,
        148
Blocher, Henri, 181, 182, 183, 188
Bonhoeffer, Dietrich, 85
Bruce, F. F., 87
Brunner, Emil, 160, 183

Calvin, John, 70, 89, 90, 160, 163
Carnell, E. J., 99–100
Carroll, Lewis, 155
Chalcedonian definition, 134
Chrysostom, 76
church, 191–92
    as body of Christ, 34–35, 126–29,
        135–36
    See also ecumenism
Clapham Sect, 59
Clemens, David, 36–37
Clines, David, 20
conversion, theology of, 62–63, 186
Cowper, William, 55
creation, 18–22
    fall of, 22–23, 28
    restoration of, 15–18, 23–27, 35–
        36, 40, 122–23, 154–55,
        170–75, 187–89
    See also humanity, as image of
        God
cross, the. *See* atonement
Crow, Jim, 108, 108 n. 14

Dembélé, Youssouf, 68–69, 69 n. 7, 70 n. 10, 71 n. 13
Descartes, René, 38–39
Dillard, Annie, 169
Dodd, C. H., 71

ecumenism, 60–61
Edwards, Jonathan, 54, 59, 64
Eißler, Tobias, 76–77
Enlightenment, 38–39, 47
Erickson, Millard, 109
eschatology, 16–17, 18, 36, 98, 111–13, 127, 134
    See also creation, restoration of; heaven
ethics, 36–37, 78, 91
Eusebius, 75
evangelism and social concern, 43–47, 99–100
exodus, the, 100–104
    See also creation, restoration of

feminist theology, 130 n. 20, 131, 133–36, 161–63
Feuerbach, Ludwig, 121
Fletcher-Louis, Crispin, 25–26
Foucault, Michel, 53
Fox, Selena, 157
Furz, John, 55

Girard, René, 80, 80 n. 37
Gnosticism, 38, 154, 161
Gonzàlez, Justo, 96–97
Gorman, Michael, 128, 134 n. 30
grace, 180, 182, 183
Graham, Billy, 70
Green, Garrett, 121
Grimshaw, William, 62–63
Gunkel, Herman, 16
Gunton, Colin, 122

Hamilton, Victor, 83
han, 105–7, 107 n. 12, 113
Harnack, Adolf von, 75
heaven
    as the New Jerusalem, 40, 138–47
    significance of for present, 147–52
Hebrews, Epistle to the, 80 n. 37, 135 n. 31

Heidegger, Martin, 16
Hindmarsh, Bruce, 182, 183, 188, 189–90
Holy Spirit, 21, 29, 33, 34, 36, 88, 110–12, 125–26, 125 n. 13, 190
Homer, 37
Horsch, John, 44
Hosea, Book of, 107 n. 12
Houston, James, 22
humanity
    as embodied, 15, 21, 40–41, 51–56, 73 n. 16, 132–36, 132 nn. 25, 26, 189–90
    fall of, 22–23, 27–28
    as image of God, 15, 18, 19–22, 23–27, 180–81
        distorted understanding of, 119–22
        male and female together, 123 n. 10, 126–36, 128 n. 15, 132 n. 24
        renewal of, 29–37, 115–16, 122–36, 124 n. 11, 125 nn. 12, 13
    See also creation, restoration of; Jesus Christ, as new Adam
Hutton, Ronald, 158, 159

Irenaeus, 74–75, 74–75 n. 21
Israel, 16–18, 23–32, 35

Jesus Christ
    as Agnus Victor, 89–91
    as Christus Victor, 67, 70–71, 72 n. 15, 78, 84–89
    as deliverer from oppression, 104–7
    incarnation of, 132–36
    as justifier, 75–76 n. 26
    as new Adam, 29, 31–34, 123–26, 124 n. 11, 125 n. 12, 131 n. 22, 132–36, 135 n. 31
Johnson, Elizabeth, 120 n. 4
justification, 75–76 n. 26, 88
    by faith, 193–94
    See also atonement, as penal substitution

Keller, Tim, 140, 141, 144
Kim, John T., 105
kingdom of God, 44, 44 n. 1, 48–49,
    58–59, 106–7, 112–13
Kline, Meredith, 19

Lackington, James, 50
Laertius, Diogenes, 129
Lausanne Committee for World
    Evangelization, 43–44, 44
    n. 1
Lavington, George, 54
law, the, 24–25, 32, 73–77
Levertov, Denise, 168–69
Lewis, C. S., 139–40, 171–75, 183
liberation theology, 95–97, 100
Long, Kathryn Teresa, 98 n. 2
Luther, Martin, 46–47, 68, 73–74, 76–
    77, 89, 119

MacIntyre, Alasdair, 194
Manicheanism, 155
Mantineia, Diotima, 159
Marcion, 74
Marrou, Henri-Irénée, 75–76 n. 26
McDowell, Edward, 143
Melton, Gordon, 156 n. 2
Methodism, 49–50, 57, 60
    See also Wesley, John
modernity, 39, 65
Moody, Dwight L., 45, 98 n. 2

natural theology, 119–22, 159–63,
    173, 173 n. 27
Newbigin, Lesslie, 153
New Testament, 36–37, 72 n. 14, 77,
    79, 80 n. 37, 123
Newton, John, 55–58, 60–61, 63
Nicene Creed, 137, 141
Nietzsche, Friedrich, 39, 40
Nordling, Cherith Fee, 180, 186–88

Old Testament, 36–37, 71, 79 n. 35,
    80 n. 37, 109, 123, 123 n. 9,
    142, 148
Oliver, Mary, 167–68
Olivers, Thomas, 57

oppression. *See* humanity, image of
    God, male and female to-
    gether; salvation, as trans-
    formation of society
Origen, 75–76

Packer, J. I., 69, 69 n. 7
Pal, Krishna, 87 n. 45
paganism
    as neo-paganism, 155–59
    relation to Christianity, 159–75
pantheism, 167 n. 19
Park, Andrew Sung, 105, 107, 107
    n. 12
Paul, the apostle, 72 n. 14, 74, 119
    n. 2, 163–67
perfectionism, doctrine of, 62–63
Philo, 19
pietism, 47, 56, 61
Piper, John, 150
postmodernity, 96
Proverbs, Book of, 66
Pseudo-Macarius, 66

Rauschenbusch, Walter, 44
Reid, Daniel G., 72 n. 14, 87 n. 44, 88
    n. 47
Renaissance, 38
Revelation, Book of, 80, 140, 143
Rivière, Jean, 75
Ruether, Rosemary Radford, 120–21

salvation
    corporate, 56–58, 65, 109–11, 117–
        18
    and ecclesiology, 60–61
    individualistic conception of, 47,
        56, 64–66, 97–100, 106, 106
        n. 11, 116–18, 181
    teleological conception of, 62–63,
        186–87
    as transformation of society, 48–
        51, 58–66, 104–13, 181,
        189–90
    See also atonement; creation, res-
        toration of; eschatology;
        heaven, as the New City;
        humanity

Sankey, Ira, 45
Satan, 77–78
    defeat of, by Christ, 84–91
    personhood of, 73 n. 16
    power of, 79–84
    reality of, 71–73, 72 nn. 14, 15
Shaftesbury, Lord 46
Sheridan, Richard, 60
Sherman, Amy, 181, 186, 191
Sider, Ronald, 109
sin, 22–23, 27–28, 79–84, 119–21
    corporate, 109–11
Smith, Christian, 109–10
social gospel, 44, 98
Socrates, 79, 129–30
Spurgeon, Charles H., 70
Starhawk, 159
Stoicism, 37–38, 40
Stott, John, 43, 68–69, 166–67
Stuhlmueller, Carol, 30

Thompson, E. P., 51 n. 21
Thompson, Greg, 146–47
Thornton, Henry, 60

Tillich, Paul, 72 n. 15
Trinity, the, 73 n. 16, 118, 119, 132
    n. 23, 192–93

Van Ruler, Arnold A., 111

Waits, Tom, 116–17
Walsh, John, 51
Walsh, Thomas, 55
Warfield, B. B., 73
Warrior, Robert Allen, 100–103
Watts, Isaac, 58
Watts, Rikk, 104 n. 8, 123 n. 9, 181,
        183, 186, 187, 188
Wesley, Charles, 48, 62
Wesley, John, 46–66
Whitefield, George, 49, 55, 57, 60–61,
        64
Wicca, 158–59
Wilberforce, William, 46, 59–60
Wilkinson, Loren, 130, 183, 187
Wordsworth, William, 157
Wright, Tom, 125 n. 12

Scripture Index

Genesis
1 36
1:2 29
1:2–9 16
1:11–12 30
1:21–25 30
1:26 24
1:26–27 20, 119, 123 n. 9
2:2–3 19
3 81, 146
3:6 25
3:17–18 22
4:4–12 22
4:23–24 22
5:1 119
5:1–2 123 n. 9, 123 n. 10, 124
5:2 132
5:3 24
6:1–6 22
7:11 19
8:2 19
8:22 165
11:1–9 144
11:4 144
15 146
32:30 146
37 23 n. 22

Exodus
3 146
3:8 24
3:17 24
4:11 29
4:22 24
13 146
14:19–21 16
14:19–31 24
19:6 26
20–23 101
20:8 26
22:21 101
23:9 27 n. 37
23:12 27 n. 38
25 146

Leviticus
19:33–34 27 n. 37
25:40 27 n. 37
25:43 27 n. 37
26:34–35 27 n. 38
26:43 27 n. 38

Numbers
20:24–28 23 n. 22

Deuteronomy
3:24 32
4:5–8 26
4:28 28
4:31 32 n. 51
4:34 32
5:13–15 27 n. 37
5:14–15 27 n. 38
6:8 25
7–9 101
10:17–19 27 n. 37
11:18 25
11:26 25
15:13–15 27 n. 37
23:7 27 n. 37
24:17–18 27 n. 37
28:12 19
28:48 28
30:3 32 n. 51
30:11–20 25
32:6 32 n. 51

Joshua
7 109

1 Samuel
2:6 83
2:8 19

2 Samuel
6:20–22 23
7:14 22 n. 21
22:8 18
22:16 18
24:1 82

1 Kings
6:20 36 n. 59
9:3 146
11:30–31 23 n. 22
19:19–21 23 n. 22

2 Kings
2 151
2:19–22 150
7:2 19

1 Chronicles
21:1 82

2 Chronicles
3:8 36 n. 59
7:14 109

Nehemiah
1:6–7 109

Job
1 82
1:16 81
1:19 81
9:6 19
9:8 19
26:11 19
28:28 25
33:4 21 n. 18
34:14 21 n. 18
38 18
38:4–6 18
38:8 18
38:10 18
38:22 18, 19

Psalms
2:7 22 n. 21
2:82 22 n. 21
8 135 n. 31
8:3–9 21
8:4–5 21
11:4 19
11:6 28
18:15 18
19 154
19:1 161
19:4 154
19:7–8 25
19:20 154
24:8 71
27 146
33:7 19
44:1–3 32
46:9 148
65:6 32
68:6 28

72 148
72:2–4 148
75:3 19
82:5 18
93 24
102:25 18, 19
103:19 19
104:2 19
104:3 19
104:5 18
106:8 32
107:24 32
109:6 82
110:10 25
111:4 32 n. 51
112:4 32 n. 51
115 28
119 32
132:9 29
132:16 29
132:18 29
135 28
135:7 19
145:8 32 n. 51
146:5–9 29

Proverbs
8:29 18
8:36 83
9:10 25
9:18 83
20:12 25

Ecclesiastes
3:10–11 169

Isaiah
1:19 25
2:1–5 30
2:20 29
3:24 28
5 27
5:1–4 28
5:8 28
5:11 28
5:18 28
5:20 28

5:21 28
5:30 28
6 27, 28
6:11–12 28
10:4 28
17:7–8 29
19:22–25 30
20:2–4 28
22:21 23 n. 22
23:18 29
24:18 18, 19
26:19 29
27:9 29
27:10 28
30:22 29
31:7 29
32:1–5 148
32:12–14 28
32:15 29, 30
35 31
35:5–6 29, 30
40–55 25
40:3 31
40:12 19
40:22 19
42:1–7 30
42:5 19, 21 n. 18
42:7 29
42:16 29, 32
44:3 29
44:6–22 25
44:24 19
45:8 29
45:12 19
45:17 29
45:18 29, 30
45:22 30
46:1–13 25
46:13 29
47:2 28
48:13 19
49:6 30
49:10 32 n. 51
49:13 32 n. 51
49:15 32 n. 51
49:24 31
50:4–5 25
51:3 30

51:13 18, 19
51:16 18
52:1 29
52:13–53:12 77
53 32, 32 n. 49, 125
54:8 32 n. 51
54:10 32 n. 51
54:11–14 142
54:13 142
54:14 142
55:7 32 n. 51
57:16 21 n. 18
58 27
59:15–21 36
59:21 29
61 31
61:1 125
61:1–2 31, 104
61:10 29
63:1–6 36
64:10 28
65:21–23 30

Jeremiah
4:23–26 28
5:21 28
7:1–29 27
7:33 28
9:10–11 28
10:12 19
10:13 19
10:14 21
19:7–9 28
22:6 28
31:37 19
32:17 19
50:25 19
51:15 19
51:16 19

Lamentations
2:20–21 28

Ezekiel
6:4 28
10 28
11:19 29

12:2 28
16:10–13 25
16:16–18 25
18:5–18 27
19:10–14 28
23:29 28
36:35 30
37 29, 30
37:5–6 29
42:16–20 36 n. 59
45:2 36 n. 59
45:2–3 36
47:7–10 30
47:9–10 31

Daniel
2 29
7 29
7:2 29
9 110

Hosea
2:3 28
2:9 28

Joel
2:3 28, 30
2:28–29 129
3:18 31

Amos
2:16 28
9:6 19
9:13 31

Micah
1:2–3 19
3 110

Habakkuk
2:19 21

Zechariah
3 88
3:2 88
3:3–5 29

3:4 83, 88
3:5 88
3:8 88
3:9 88
12:1 18, 19
14:14 29

Malachi
3:10 19

**Wisdom
of Ben Sira**
17:1–13 123 n. 9
49:16–50:1 26

**Wisdom
of Solomon**
2:23 123 n. 9
2:24 82 n. 39
19:6 24

Matthew
3:11 125 n. 13
3:11–12 33
4:1–11 85
4:3 79
4:8 79–80
4:23 125
5–7 32
6:9–13 140
7:12 37
9:36 32 n. 51
10:40–42 33 n. 52
11:2–6 31
12:48–50 33 n. 52
14:14 32 n. 51
15:32 32 n. 51
16:24–25 126
18:27 32 n. 51
20:34 32 n. 51
21:14 33
24:37 16
25:31–46 33 n. 52
27:33–56 77 n. 32

Mark
1:7–8 33
1:41 32 n. 51

2:27 32
3:22–27 31
3:27 70, 85
6:34 32 n. 51
8:2 32 n. 51
8:14–10:52 32
9:33–10:45 33
10:45 32, 32 n. 49
10:46–52 33
12:28–34 37

Luke

3:15–16 33
4 31, 104, 106
4:13 85
4:18 125
4:18–19 104
4:24–27 104
6:35–36 128 n. 15
7:13 32 n. 51
7:18–23 31
9:23 107
10:18 85
10:29 128 n. 15
10:33 32 n. 51
13:10–16 81 n. 38
13:16 81 n. 38
15:20 32 n. 51
16:15 128 n. 15
18:9 128 n. 15
20 128 n. 15
20:34–36 133
20:35 133
20:36 133
22:31 83
22:32 83
23:47 124 n. 11

John

1:1 31
1:1–2 123
1:12–13 134 n. 29
1:14 31, 123
1:17 32
1:29 71, 89
1:36 71
3:1–8 118

3:5 134 n. 29
5:15–23 31
8:31–32 85
8:34 85
8:44 79, 85
11:38 31
12:31 70, 81, 85
14:8–11 31
14:15–27 33
16:5–15 33
16:11 70
18:37 86
20:22 33

Acts

1 140
2 50
2:14–36 135
10:38 81, 81 n. 38
14 165
14:15–17 166
17 183
17:24 167
17:24–31 121
17:27 167
17:28 124 n. 11, 167

Romans

1 35, 165, 183
1:19 165
1:20 160
3:21–26 77
3:26 90
5 34, 132
5:9–11 36
5:12 81, 82
5:12–19 33
5:12–21 122, 124,
   124 n. 11
6:17 85
7–8 88
7:12 32
7:14 32
7:23 80
8 118, 128, 132
8:1 88
8:2 88

8:3 88
8:12–17 34
8:15–17 36
8:19–21 35
8:20 81
8:29 126
8:32 125
8:38 72
12:1–2 127
12:2 126

1 Corinthians

1:18 36
1:27 146
2:6–9 72 n. 14
2:6–16 34
3 146
3:16–18 136
3:21–23 136
6:12–17 133
7:31 127
11:7 123
12–14 34
12:9 34
12:13–14 128
12:24–26 128
15 135
15:3 77
15:21–22 33
15:45–49 33
15:49 124
15:56 84

2 Corinthians

3:18 34, 124
4:4 33, 123
4:6 34
5:11–21 77
5:17 34, 134
5:21 125
11:3 79
11:14–15 80

Galatians

2:20 126
3:1–5 34
3:13 88 n. 47

3:14 34
3:23 87
3:26–29 127
3:28 35
4:6 34
5 128
5:16 34
5:16–26 34
5:25 126
6:2 126
6:15 34
6:15–16 35
6:16 134 n. 30

Ephesians
1:4 138
1:4–5 122
1:9–10 122
1:11–12 138
1:18 138
1:18–23 34
2:5 36
2:6 34, 137
2:7 138
2:8 36
2:10 34, 138
2:15 138
4–6 34
4:1–5 35
4:5–6 136
4:13 124 n. 11
4:14 79
4:15 138
5:10–20 36

Philippians
2:1–8 131
2:1–16 35
2:1–18 34
2:7 126
2:8 86

Colossians
1:4–5 150
1:13 137
1:15 33, 34, 121, 123
1:16 72

1:17 167
1:18 34
1:19–20 123
2:11 87 n. 44
2:14 87 n. 44
2:14–15 86
2:15 70, 87 n. 44, 90
3:9–11 127

1 Thessalonians
1:10 138
3:5 79
5:9 138

1 Timothy
3:6 83
6:13 86
6:19 138

2 Timothy
2:26 79
3:5 80

Hebrews
1:1–3 77
1:3 123
1:9–10 77
2:9 123
2:9–10 135 n. 31
2:14 83, 87
2:14–15 70
2:15 83, 90
3:3 69 n. 7
4:1–11 34
4:9–11 138
4:14–8:13 34
5:9 124 n. 11
9:15 87
9:22 87–88
9:27–28 88
11:8–10 150
11:9–12 143
11:16 145
12:2 124 n. 11

James
3:9 123
4:4 81
5:14–18 34

1 Peter
1:4 138
1:22 85
2:4–5 34
5:8 83

2 Peter
3:6–7 16

1 John
2:1 124 n. 11
2:14 85
2:18–27 80
3:7 124 n. 11
3:8 70, 149
5:19 81

Jude
6 72

Revelation
2:26 147
3 145
3:8 145
3:12 143, 144
3:21 147
5 71, 89, 147
5:5 71
5:6 89
5:9 89
5:10 147
7:9 113
12 87
12:9 79
12:10 82
12:11 87
17:14 71
20:2 79
21:1–2 140
21:2–5 36
21:12–14 142
21:15–27 36
21:22 36
22 141
22:1–3 152
22:4 144